# *intersections* of concern

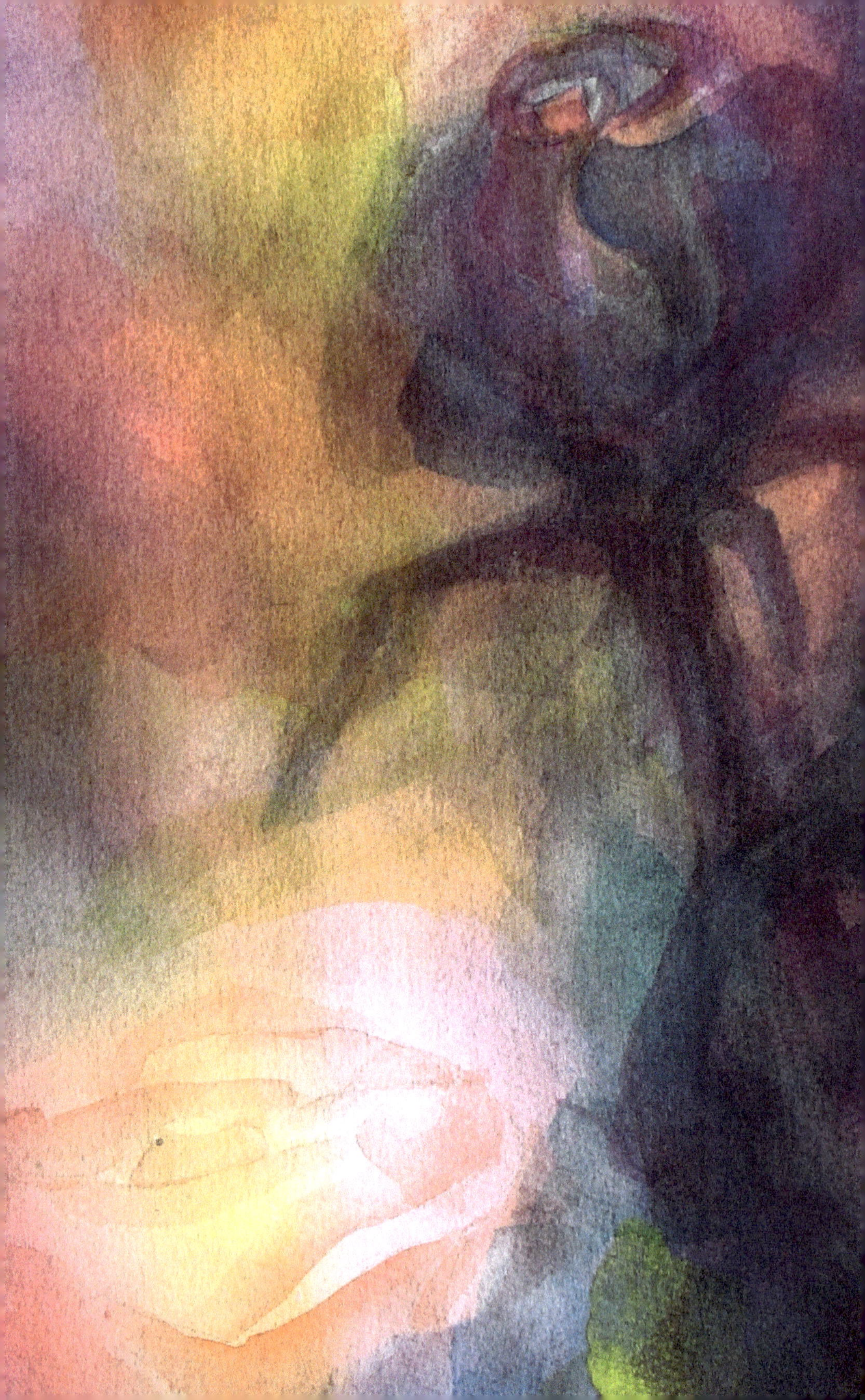

# *intersections of concern*

prose poems and images

Rainer Neumann

Published by

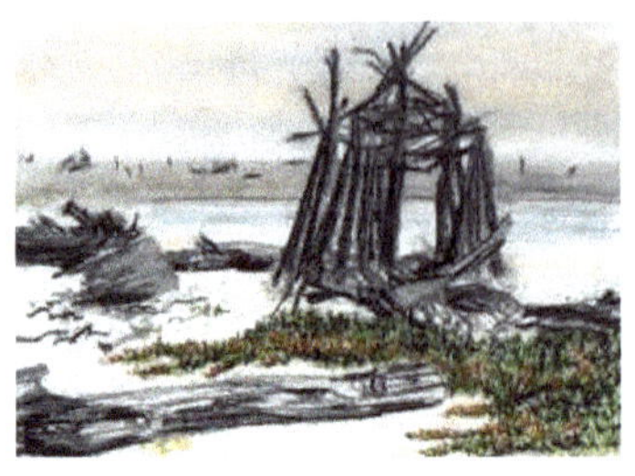

landseandsky



ISBN 978-0-578-72898-8

Cover and interior images (pastels, photographs, watercolors) are by the author except as noted.

For printed works and ebooks go to:

lulu.com/spotlight/rneumann

All other inquiries email:

onhighwayone@gmail.com

Or visit my website:

landseandsky.com

# dedication

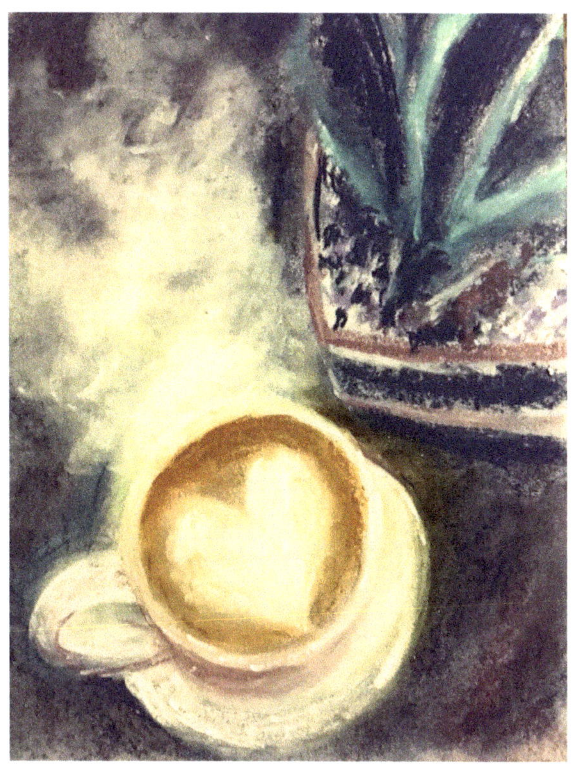

to Harpo
for his
generosity

to Clifford
for his poetic
inspiration

to Barbara
for her
support


# acknowledgements

thanking
those who continue to search for truth in the midst
of overwhelming world events
those who support the freedoms needed to bring
justice and opportunity to our
diverse communities
those who open their hearts and minds to inspire
the next generation…

## contents

dedication

acknowledgments

preface 10

introduction 12

*let the words go deep 12*

journeys 15

*only existence 16*

*alleyways of Barcelona 19*

*Istanbul 21*

*a cock crows 23*

*back at work 27*

*ruins 28*

*twilight walk 30*

*a pilgrimage 32*

suddenly a pandemic 41

*life to come 42*

*solitude 45*

*live stream from Bogotá 48*

*a hawk 51*

*still we live 59*

tragedy and resilience 65

*beating hearts 66*

*the flames 68*

*spirals of fury 72*

*day of solitude 75*

*we can change 77*

*somewhere 78*

*for the sake of family 80*

*contradictions 83*

*to begin again 85*

*the depths 89*

contents


struggle and democracy 91

*a voice 92*

*refugees 93*

*all the years 98*

*transcending borders 101*

*days of revolution 104*

*a new democracy 109*

*thoughts of freedom forming*

*to write 113*

awareness and joy 117

*in the midst 118*

*the tide 119*

*knight of mirrors 122*

*we are 124*

*ode to mountain joy 128*

*something still burns 130*

postlude 134

*the word becoming 134*

hopes and dreams *138*

other works *140*


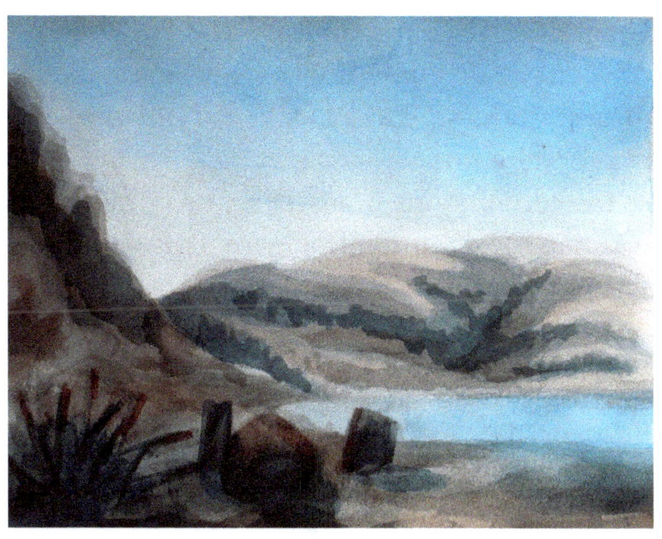

# preface

*written in the midst of fears, sacrifice and resilience*

a pandemic has come into our lives
the world wide web of information
  spews out the news
a few infected people traveling
back to their homes from around the world
some with symptoms some testing positive
several countries have a growing number
of people contacted by this invisible scourge
this protein molecule that invades our oxygen cells
emergency reactions precautions taken
hospitals filling up infected people dying
    not enough masks supplies ventilators
    becoming the difference between death and recovery
sheltering in place and social distancing is
becoming the norm and necessity around the world
not knowing how long it will last or
    how virulent it will be...
it has reached into America into our neighborhoods
our families our selves...
so sudden...
coming after a litany of tragic situations
that so many are still contending with...
    the ravages of fires in Santa Rosa and Paradise
    the innocent deaths of children shot in schools
    the innocent fans shot at a Las Vegas concert
and now as I write this
we are in the convulsions of anger and protests prompted
by a black man dying under the knee of a white police
officer - "I can't breath" - becoming the flashpoint of a
continuing social and political reality that has surfaced
again in America and in the world...

these are all life changing situations, social, cultural and authoritarian realities tragically brought home to
a loved one a family a mother son father daughter and
the larger communities we live in

and yet within all this turmoil and tragedy the over whelming resilience of people still rises up and
continues to rise up...
to ultimately respond and organize and demand equal
justice under our laws...
to ultimately help bring about equal opportunities
for all people...

it is in this regard and at this time that I want to share this compilation of poems and images created over the last few years...they not only come out of late night anguish and heartfelt thoughts but they are also in response to our jubilant and joyful existence - twilight walks through a eucalyptus grove, intimate jazz music on Friday nights, magnificent sunsets, inspiring conversations and exhibits at the local cafes, the enriching diversity of our world communities and our unique experience on this earth...

hopefully some of the poems and images will go deep,
fill up your hearts and lift up your thoughts...

June 15, 2020

*our lives upside down*
*light and shadow coincide*
*we will find our way*

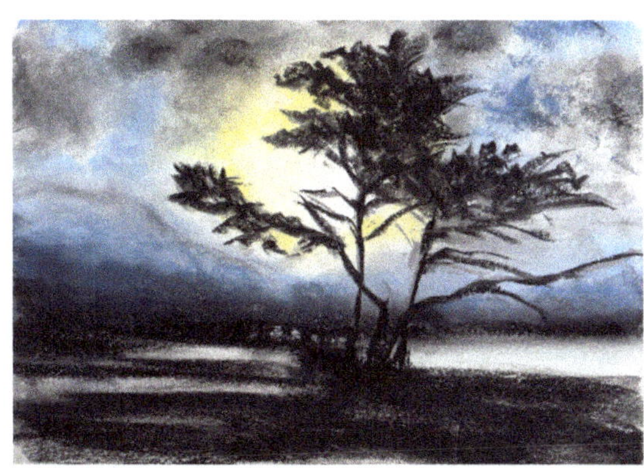

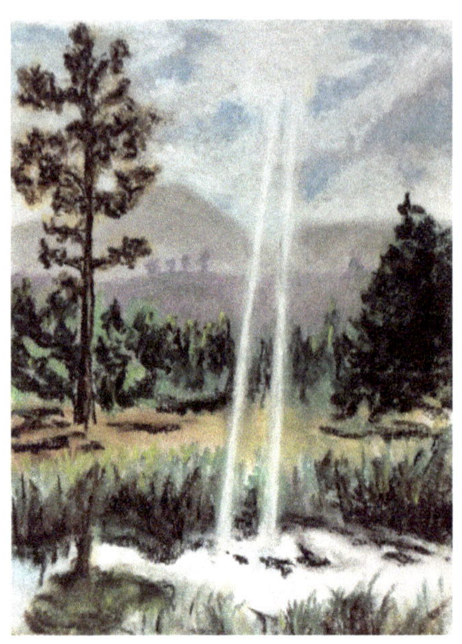

# introduction

*let the words go deep*

let the words go deep
to meet the source
of their existence

let them drink from the
sacred springs of meaning

and ignite the eruption
of language

let the words resonate in the memory of your mind
within all you have come to know
within all you have come to be

let the words take on
all you are capable of grasping and
embracing
pull a sword out of your smart phone
reach for a ring in the darkness
take up the gauntlet of comments
revere honor in these times of
ignominious tweets and retweets
uproot the ruination of language and
respect

let the words overcome
all your disillusioned thoughts
all your nihilistic tendencies
let the words transcend
all your existential fears
of the unforgiving
unrelenting eternal night

let words of concern
strike a chord of what is needed
Let them move you
inspire you
infuse you
with an inner resolve to be
strong in the armor of
what you think is right

let the desire of words
become you
all over again and again
and when you are spent and
aching barely breathing grasping reaching
hard for something to still believe in

dive deeper into the vortex
of words that swirl around you
submerge and emerge
out of the waters of
cleansing and imagination

remember one thing
that gives you meaning
give this a word
fill it with life

remember some one
who gives you meaning
who has entered your heart
give them a word
fill them with love

I have my own something
my own someone
that my words hold onto
you have yours

*but its time to travel*
*to  remember*
*to take my staff*
*    my windbreaker*
*    my knapsack*
*into an open mind field*
*on a path that seems right*

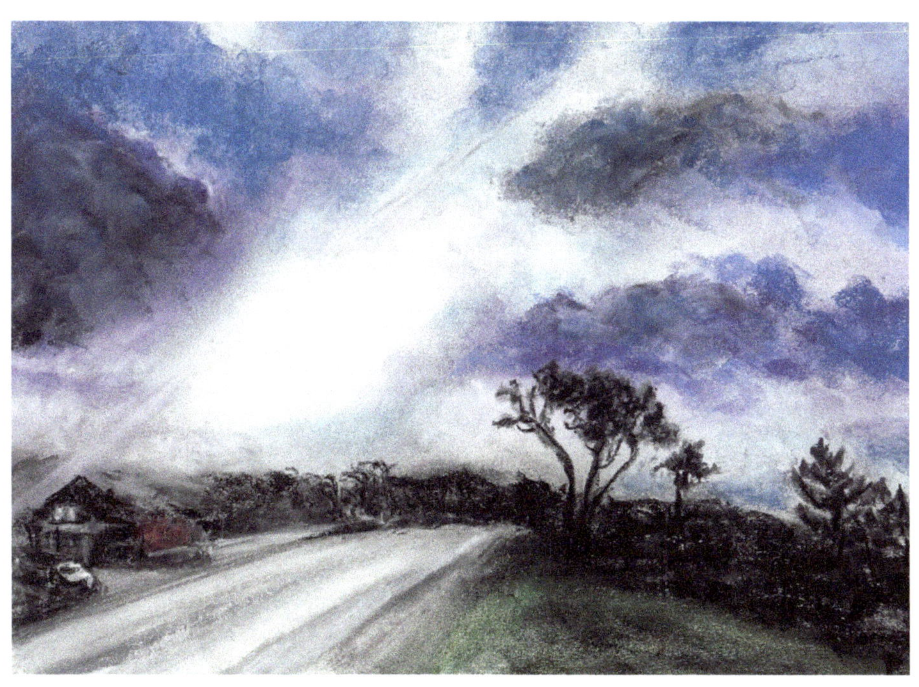

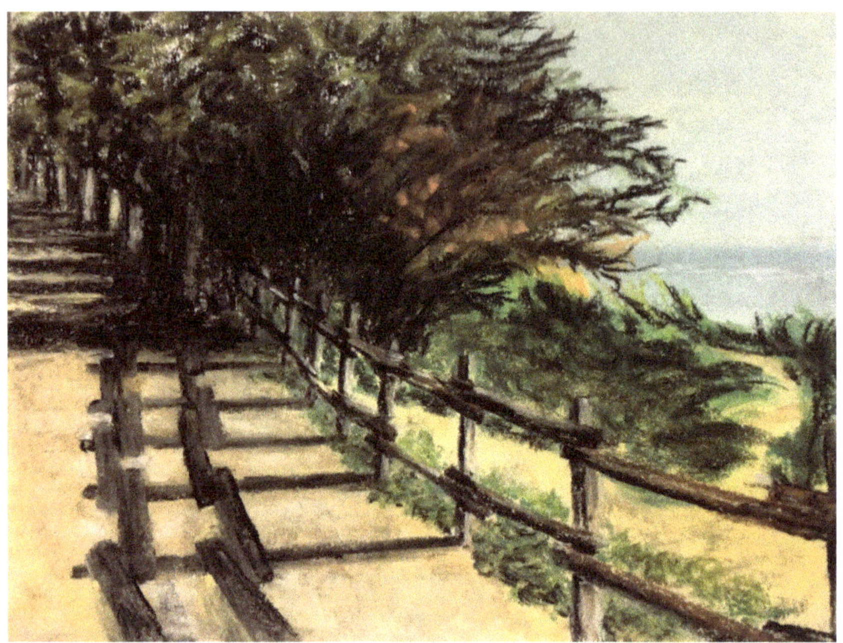

it's time to travel
to wander
to lay my fate
beyond the gate
on a path
that seems right

the world
has no religion for me
no ideology
no borders
that I know of
at least in my mind
my heart or the sky

only existence
has come to me
on this small blue orb
somewhere in some town
along the coast
somewhere in the dark
star lit moon lit night
of the universe
in this short time zone
of breathing and feeling
between the sunrise and the moon

only existence
for a man in his time
not looking for salvation
not climbing a mountain top
or sitting in a cave of isolation
or claiming nirvana

but it's time to travel
to remember
to take my staff
    my wind breaker
    my knapsack
into an open mind field
on a path that seems right

the world
is all that has seduced me excited me
the past the history the layers of life
the endeavors the notions the prairie houses
the pilgrimage the visions seen
    the dreams attempted
the love in every night time and
    the life in my remembered eyes

the world
I grew up in
has passed and yet remains
with the deaths I had no part in
the refugees we took in
running from the soldiers incensed
    hungry and looking for young women
    the spoils of the victors
    the razing of the towns cities and land

only existence
is what reaches out to me
envelopes me
touches me
goes into time traveling
time being
wander lust is just
setting my fate
beyond the gates
over the fences
around the walls
imagined passports
becoming thresholds of fields forests
lonesome highways grand canyons
quaint cafes

its time to travel
to wander
to lay my fate
beyond the gate
on a path
that seems right

## *alleyways of Barcelona*

I was overcome
by a brutal act
the violence
the pain of loss
a memorial
on Las Ramblas
had taken me close to the
alleyways
the old pathways of
Barcelona

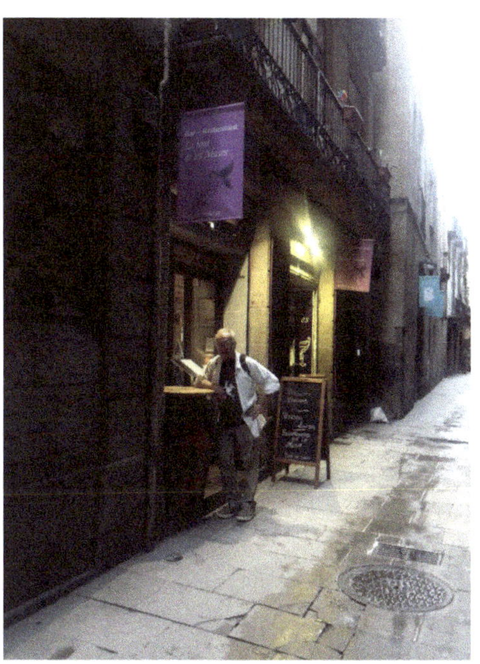

photograph by Barbara Neumann

she was walking
past the doorways
local murals
faded colors
with knowing eyes
she drew me in
so I followed her down the alleyways
to escape into the belly of Barcelona

the walls of stone
six stories high
shadows reaching
out of the past
it was either live
or slowly die
so I followed her down the alleyways
for redemption in Barcelona

I was hungry
and she knew it
not for tapas
or sangria
I was lost
and needed comfort
so I followed her down the alleyways
to be my savior in Barcelona

I heard dancers
and hands clapping
guitars echoed
off the walls
reminding me of my
path and calling
as she led me down the alleyways
to be my muse in Barcelona

then night closed in
cafes shut down
the moon shone through
the stones above
and let us breathe
in light and love
we found a place in the alleyways
deep in the heart of Barcelona

healing the heart in Barcelona

# *Istanbul*

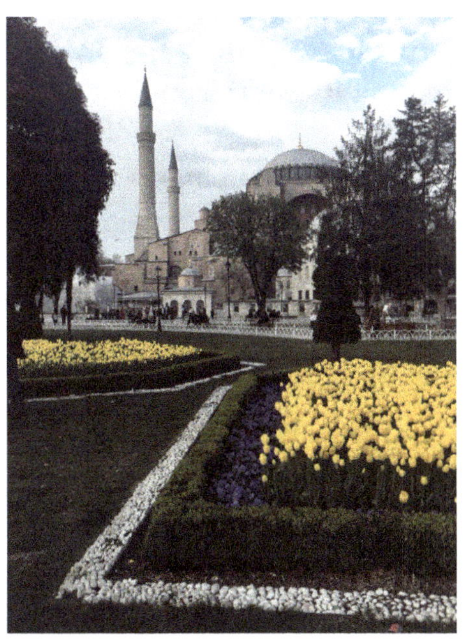

Istanbul
your place in history is
intact founded in
antiquity
the walls of your memory
are in states of decline
and construction
the streets and the
alleyways
embrace the steps of your
ancestors
before Jesus walked
around Galilee

your water brought the traders and the raiders
and eventually the walls of such formidable strength
that palaces were built and mythologies became real

the Hagia Sophia overwhelming in its domed beauty
and many centuries later
the Blue Mosque infused with prayer five times a day

feeling secure
in the words of the last chant
amplified by speakers in the minarets
fitting into the mold of your traditions
wearing the clothes of your beliefs

Istanbul
your place of traditions was remade by Atatürk
in the upheaval of modern history
in the neighborhoods the antique stores
still auctioning your artifacts
the alleyways of bakeries and cafes

metro lines connecting the old with the high-rise
the ancient markets the baths that take off the old skin
the remaining Christian churches with their icons
    and madonnas
reminders of that earlier spiritual birth and path
overtaken by Mohammed's swords in the 15th century
becoming an empire where black slaves
in their physical glory ruled within the confines
of the concubines for the pleasures of the sultans

    the Hagia Sophia overwhelming in its domed beauty
        and many centuries later
    the Blue Mosque infused with prayer five times a day

feeling secure
in the words of the last chant
amplified by speakers in the minarets
fitting into the mold of your traditions
wearing the clothes of your beliefs

Istanbul
your hospitality found us in an area called Batal
    in a room called Melissa
an older building remodeled in a
    most modern style
by the owner and engineer
    called Emil
whose daughter in law lovingly
    prepared our breakfast
    of olives bread cheese cucumber
    and Turkish tea
our words of good morning echoed
    in the warmth of their company

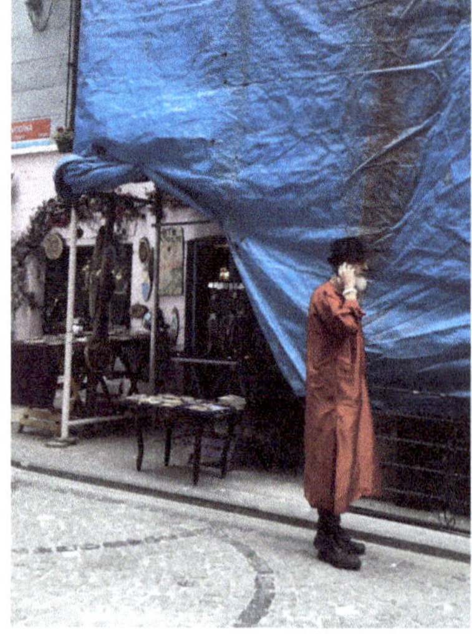

feeling secure fitting into the mold
    of their traditions

## *a cock crows*

*a desultory morning outside of Nairobi*

a cock crows
above the noise of three wheeled tuk tuks
taking someone around the potholes and the ruts
up down the road
stop for a stranger hop on board
any more than three's a crowded load

a dog barks
scooters swerve to avoid and miss the lorries
two on the back with a container of water
up down the road
hang on to the straps and a waist
any more than three's a heavy load

well you've got to be careful
you can't walk this street at night
Nairobi's preserve is open out here
  the skyline is a distant silhouette
  in shadow and vague light
a backdrop for lions looking for an easy meal
  with their mane and their might
while a hidden rhino family comes onto the open
stage with five guards and guns watching for
  poachers in their sight
don't be fooled by the hippos they are the rocks
in the water and deadly with oversized jaws
while gazelles graze always in a state of alert
  beauty mixes with survival in this land
  of tooth and claws
where zebras and wildebeests leave many
hoof prints in the dirt

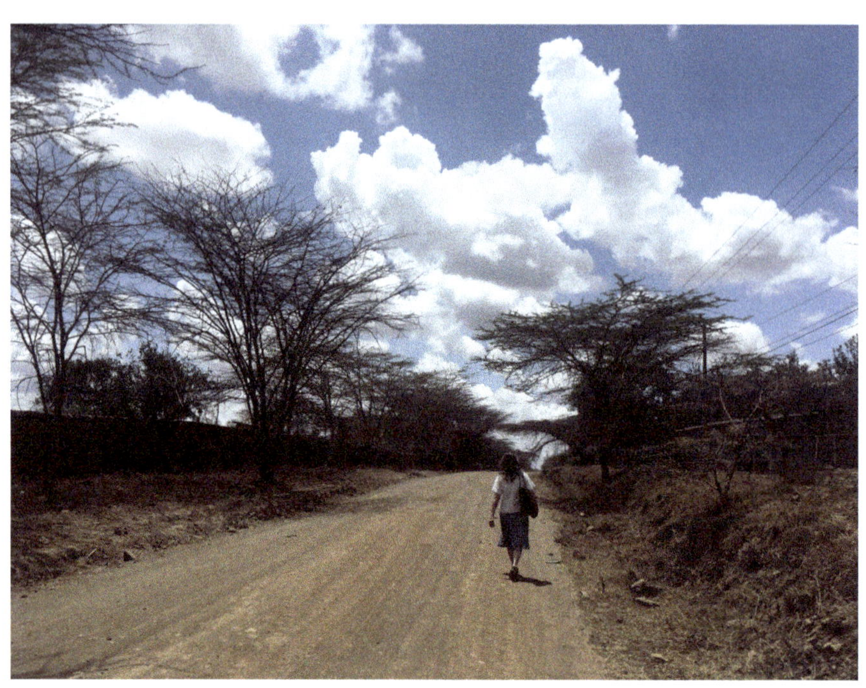

a cock crows
the sky has opened to another morning
here the clouds billow and set the scene
up down the street
flowering clothes walk with heads held high
raising dust under their feet

a bus stops
another day of enterprise comes to life
a wooden structure a corrugated roof
up down the street
time to sell what's been grown
an avocado that's surprisingly sweet

we stayed at the Osoita lodge
designed by an Indian woman
    who is also the chef in charge
and keeps the rambunctious late night
    noise makers in line
the dining hall is spacious

in the style of a grand grass shack
smiles greet us with the morning's fare
  and we feel grateful to be there
our day is to be spent at a Waldorf school
a walk up the road to celebrate 100 years
  worldwide and 30 here
a celebration for those who have worked
built and continued what once was sown
  by the endeavors of a few
for all for the children to come and see
what will be will be...

a drum pounds
there is energy and optimism
that seems to permeate the school ground
up down those attending
there is a reverence for teachers
within this walled enclosure

in the school class rooms and playground
there is singing and dancing and love you can feel
overwhelming the wild so close yet here
intentions have gathered together
children not far from the future
they are eagerly wanting to join
eagerly wanting to grasp
and take hold of the hands who reach out
they are boarded and fed and taught and readied
for the world in transition
these wide eyed children
these hearts minds and feet
adding their arts and their songs
to their primal beat

a bell rings
talk of plans at the home of a founder
tea in the afternoon an invitation
up down the arcana
drumbeats move us until we're sitting
looking over the wild savanna

a solid house built of stone
by a remembered love and left
to an engaging woman almost alone
    with a grazing eland on the lower veranda
with a caring friend who is long employed
     bringing biscuits to go with the tea
and we talk of history and changes in the country
and the school and think of times to come
looking out in a quiet moment...

so extensive the vista

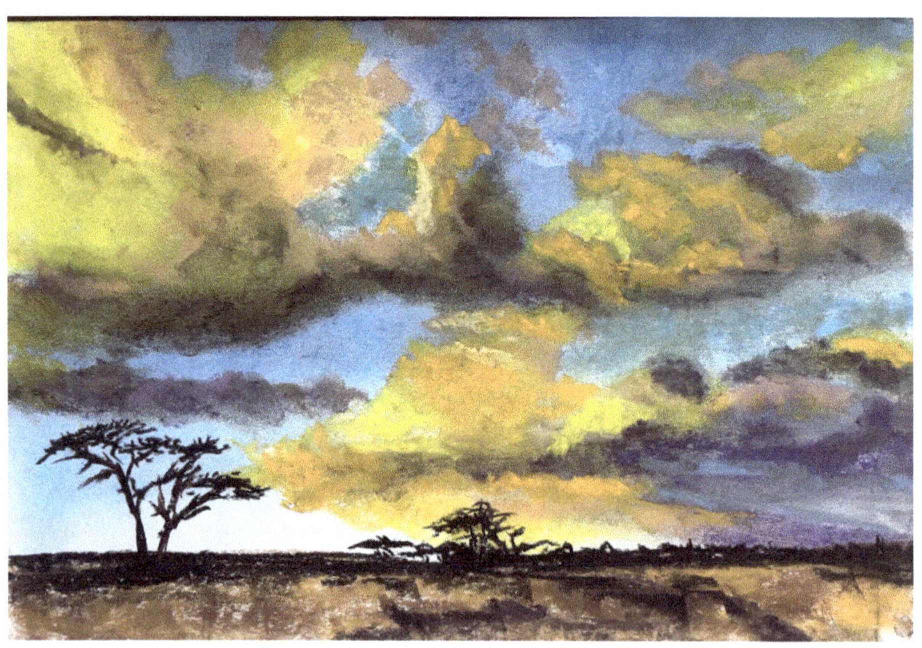

back at work
back at the coffee cafe
sorting through the words
that are never enough
the changes that I
scramble and ramble through
invoking my muse
and the elementals at play

back at the office
back at the table of comfort food
going through the pages
that I filled up and rewrote
invoking discernment
and a sober inner voice

back in the ring
back in the bout of my life
taking on the phrases in which
I buzz and counter and maneuver
invoking the odds
of my discontent and strife

back in the moment
at the cross roads of choice
seeing the landscape revealed
that has brought some joy and relief
invoking my will
and the wonder of existence

contemplating the ruins of a silo missile site
on Sweeney Ridge above Pacifica
tagged by artists who walked the trail
who saw the remains
rusted beams and fallen roof
strewn about and scattered
in a once comfortable and boring place
waiting for the inevitable
walls of cinder blocks
now covered in aerosol colors
unknown names letters outlined
expressionist faces
    painted by curious Picassos and Klees
gone beyond the imagined ghosts
there waiting and carrying on with
hikers joggers and gasping dogs

once the threat of an attack seemed real
once the defense was thought out
missiles devised and revised and
placed in the silos of semi security
men managed watchfully
twenty four hours a day
once eyeing our great Pacific coast
our cliffs and beaches for the attack
a great moat between our way of life
and the threats of destruction
    from the east

how strange to read the Spaniard's story
Portola riding close to these silos in the 16th C
viewing the bay to the east and ocean to the west
those travelers upon the ridge
those explorers from abroad

riding over a history of knowing feet
a history of living generations
cultures of life upon this giving earth
with thankfulness and reverence
to the spirit within all
and all around them

our walk has opened up our sight
from close inspection of local plants
to wind swept hills and crests

now we turn about and take in the horizon
El Diablo rears up in the east
the devil too has found a place
the bottom of the bay is in between
the tech revolution born and the valley renamed
to the fabled city of Saint Francis in the north
to San Jose in the south peninsula
now turning to face the wide horizon of
the great Pacific peacefully
waiting in waves and tides and sunset reds
today an apricot hue

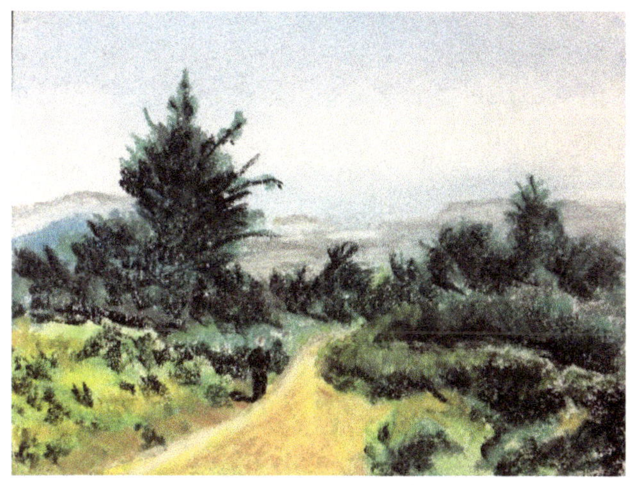

we have our
bearings
it's time
to return
to our own
findings
and future
discoveries

## *twilight walk*

through the pampas grass
the path well worn
through the eucalyptus grove
the scent filling essence infusing our memory
permeating now intoxicating
higher still the sun is setting
in an after glow of pale apricot
not wanting to let go
crests of hillsides remaining

yet we walk on
slowly immersing in the violet
of the west and the dying day
so buried in our daily time and life
and I wonder and I live
as if it will never end

just how hard is it to know the end
as so many have known it
life ending life told of endings
life written on scrolls and manuscripts
life ending in meaning and remembrance
the Rabbi's chest
carried in a sacred cadence
the coffin open
to a made up corpse
the ashes in an urn
so carefully held
so carefully taken to a redwood grove
and scattered amongst the roots and the soft earth
becoming the seeds of beginnings
some so carefully taken on a boat
and strewn into the roiling sea
amongst the waves and currents
into the mouths of the living and dying

remembering who they were
remembering who I am
remembering what was once
a man a woman a child
so brave upon this earth
with the breath of life
in the light of the stars

remembering
all the hills we climbed
the paths through pines and granite
through redwoods over streams
through glass and steel
waiting for a taxi
full of all we managed to do
all we grasped all we took on
and managed to create
the glow on my face
when the work was satisfying
and wanted and needed
in the world

at some point we walk back
closing the circle the street the grove
the aroma of the upward path
opening into the sky at twilight
the first star seen then the turn around
side stepping the way back down
        finally to the gate
between the land preserved
and the pavement borders
of the houses built and the lives being lived
back to our avenue the gardens known
back to what we left
what we left
back home

## *a pilgrimage*

*from Half Moon Bay to San Francisco*
*to a time when poets read to the rhythms of a stand up bass*
*the sticks of a drummer*
*the chords of black and white keys…*
*to a time when a howl was heard across the land*
*and one such poet heard it and let it fly*
*and made sure the world would not let it pass by*
*writing and publishing keeping the door open*
*to the spirit of human striving and loving*
*and the beatitude of our existence…*

on the 100th birthday of Lawrence Ferlinghetti
"a pilgrimage"
beginning on the path of his own words:

*"a poet walks on a high wire of his own making…"*

I sit and wonder
thinking of the hours spent
wandering up the hill stepping
one hundred ninety two steps
to the top of Nob Hill finally
able to turn around look
way down through the
theater district of odd characters
way down past Geary Street
through the old buildings
of character on the left
and the new replacements on the right
right where the Continental Bus Depot
used to be yes you didn't have to go too far
to go far just buy your ticket for
South Lake Tahoe and the day

became a possibility a life changing
ring grabbing possibility and
you settle back into your chair wondering
who is going to sit next to you

look further down
Glide Memorial is rocking
with that uplifting gospel music
lifting you higher and shifting
back and forth hallelujah lord
    *I've come to pray my rocking soul is here today*
    *hallelujah lord I'm on my way looking for a*
    *hoping for a working for a better day*
I can hear them feel them
holding hands in time
holding hands in mine
now standing on California Street
the rails are singing the chorus
of a cable car still rattling
    that once brought top hats
    and much later tie dyed skirts and t-shirts
    to Huntington Park
mommas with new borns
are now coming around and
kids dashing to the playground
young lovers sit on the benches
basking in SF cool and their warmth
    while the constant sound of falling water
    coming out of the marble mouths
    of giant fish and cherubs is heard while
    naked youth dance around this
transplanted fountain in all its bizarre
baroque glory paying homage to spring
in the midst of the plaza

I sit also and look into the western sky
and try to catch the sun before it hides
behind the bell tower of Grace Cathedral
the rose window is lit from within
and the high voices of pre-pubescent boys
comes wafting out of the front side door
    young voices singing old hymns of
    godly glory swelling the inner space
reaching upward reaching for the heavens
letting the saints of colored glass
immerse the chapel structure
the pews the worshipers
in veils of red blue and yellow
    from the sounds of rocking hallelujahs
to the sounds of lifting harmonies
I am in my skeptical way touched by
the hopeful voices that dare to include
all of "God's children" and all
of all persuasions to open up
their hearts and minds
towards a more tolerant
spirit sprouting in these times
    even as I am tolerant of the
evenings take over of the park
by every dog and loving owner
    living around the neighborhood
all seeming to be sniffing
    and accepting each other
enjoying this hour of freedom

onward I finally say
and continue north on Taylor Street
past three and four story apartment buildings
now brightening up the street with
their light and living mysteries
above the occasional restaurant

and grocery store and laundromat
their lit up lobbies reminding me
of a genteel time when apartment
dwellers could and would sit on couches
amidst still-life paintings and ferns
    in the lobby corners
    neighboring tenants communing
    inside an imagined life
looking through the ornate iron work
    of a somewhat secure front door

    and yet another ascendency
is ahead of my slow wandering gait
upward climbing to reach
the top of Russian hill
the view opens to Alcatraz in the north
and the bay bridge to the east
and the financial glass and steel
    start up deals to the south
almost forgetting Coit Tower
in between sensuous views
ready to ejaculate onto Telegraph hill
I meant hose down the city
    in case of another fire
now the steps meander down
between homes and apartments
an arboretum cared for by the inhabitants
a lit up door number in case someone is looking or
visiting lives transpiring within bay windows
and redwood doors and hardwood floors
maybe a lonely hearted clothing designer
maybe a poet or two struggling for the right words
or an artist with a glass of vermouth
    studying her latest work
or a family making sure homework
    is getting done

or friends toasting to a *"grand notion"*
or a newly published book
or a just released film soon to be
shown at Sundance
  here the old paths are forgotten
native people are barely remembered
as the waves of immigrants and
gold seekers of every persuasion came and
  built their hillside dreams
  grateful to be there
Reaching Powell Street Union Street and the Italian
delis and coffee roasters I finally find Puccini's on
Columbus with an aria from La Boheme
streaming out the door I get
a cappuccino a tiramisu and
a seat at the window looking out
on the world as it is and as it could be
excited conversations resound over the table
  until a bass voice from the
  steppes of Russia rumbles out of a corner
  and begins to sing no one minds
  the talk quiets down
  the moment is proclaimed
  pain emerges from the gut and throat
    the loss of a son
all wait and listen
the moment passes and
every life in that hallowed space
continues with a deeper connection
to our primal humanity
I nod to the singer and take my leave

walking towards Broadway
lovely ladies invite me inside
but I look further and see
the naked lady on the wall of Vesuvios

having a martini
ahh the informality of it all

an invitation I can't resist
the swinging doors the dusty
history on the walls and
the glossy tables in remembrance
of the house artist O'Shaughnessy
who once lived in the basement creating
the table top images under the varnish
ready to be perused and remembered
by those who look for such things and recognize
the subtlety of our momentary beauty
    standing with the locals at the bar
    I order a local Sierra Nevada
a striking woman is in the sedan chair
    I linger there
    and will stop in again
if time allows and death
holds off a while longer

I am somewhat weary
but must stop next door across the alley
    and step into City Lights to circle the shelf
    displays of books and magazines
and check out the latest publications
of this renowned and fearless iconoclastic bookseller

I walk amidst the reminders of the
questioning minds in print
their readings and invocations
their fight for creative imperatives
free expression heady existence
a howlful legacy to be continued
in this corner of the world
in this corner of America

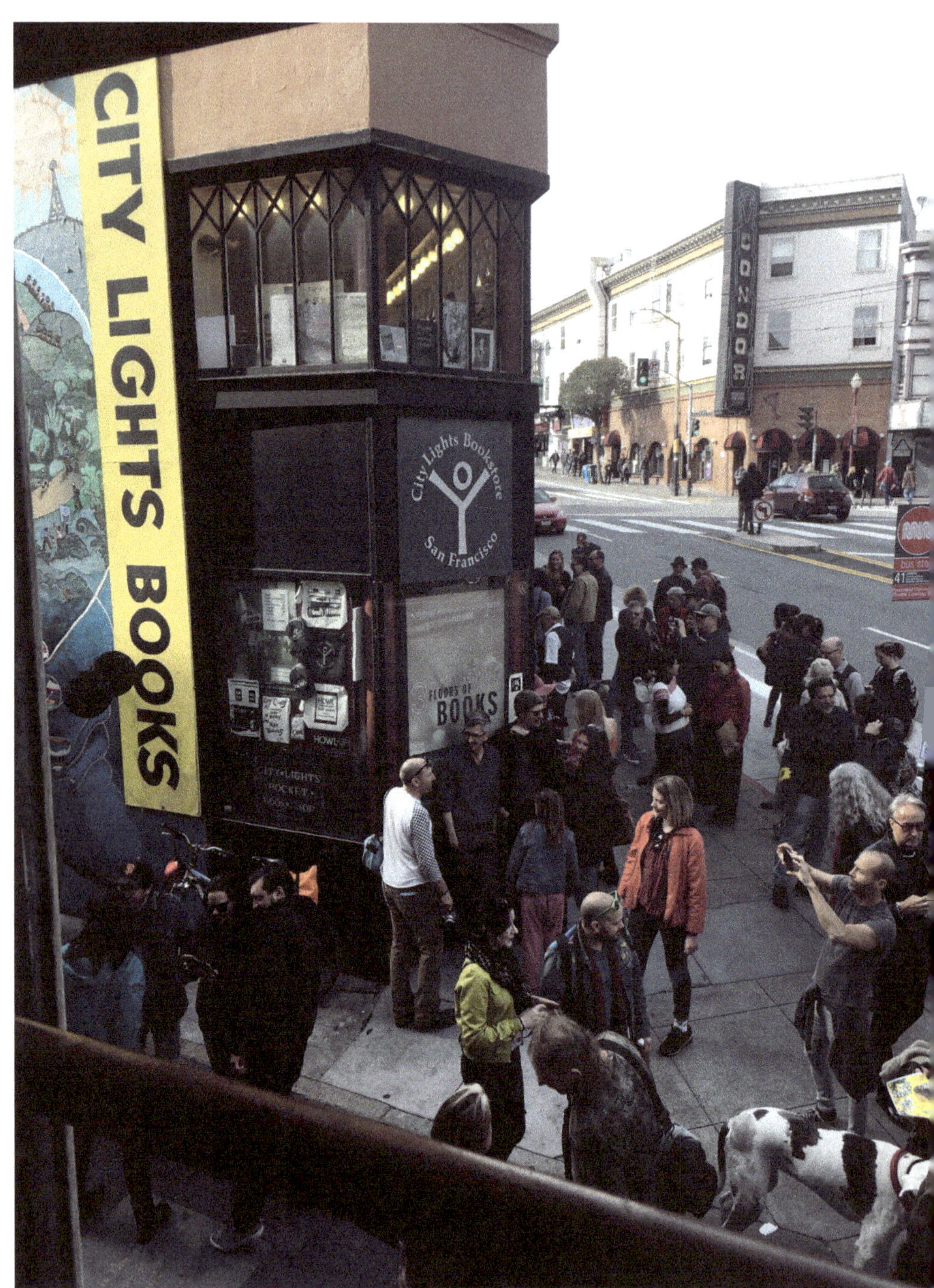
CITY LIGHTS BOOKS
City Lights Bookstore
San Francisco
FLOORS OF
BOOKS
CONDOR

the poets writers town criers
high flying towards the source
staying the course letting
their works free fall
to the searching and struggling and
questioning and wondering     yes

those still wondering what freedom means
and what it has to offer
the vigilance needed to keep light
coming through the cracks

I am in a heady state
need some air buy a small book of poetry
"*San Francisco Poems*" by
Lawrence Ferlinghetti
the night is still reeling
noisy moving with the late nighters
I am ready to hail a taxi
    and head to my place of repose
thinking on my way home
opening the book on my way homeward
    turning pages I read:

    *"Poets, come out of your closets,*
        *Open your windows, open your doors,*
        *You have been holed - up too long*
        *in your closed worlds"*

too soon too soon the tunnel is found
Sutter Street has come
remembered nuggets once found
still there here somewhere
    got to dig a lot deeper
        got to go a few more blocks
            before I sleep...

# suddenly a pandemic

*her voice like a healing spirit fills the air*
*with words of solace and gratefulness and*
*momentary soothing in this time of such an*
*unknown and misunderstood invasive threat*

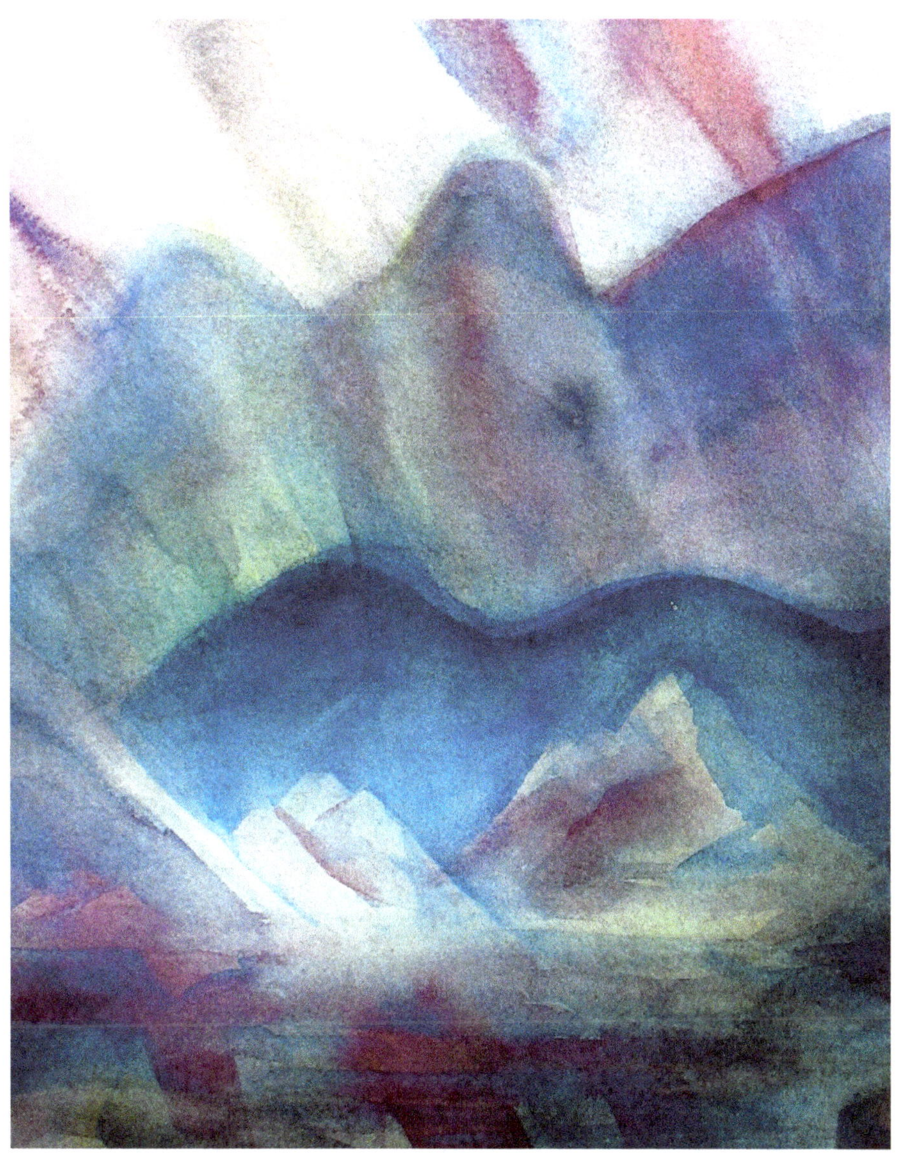

# *life to come*

a Saturday evening
walk through the eucalyptus grove
aromatic awakening
enlivening
a tune remembered in the steps
fel da ree fel da rah
such wandering
upon the soft breathing earth

for a short while
the relentless news has chilled
competing blame has stilled
a squawk breaks through the reverie
an unseen messager
upon some branch
with the cupping of an ear
and a look into the sky
I listen for the message sent

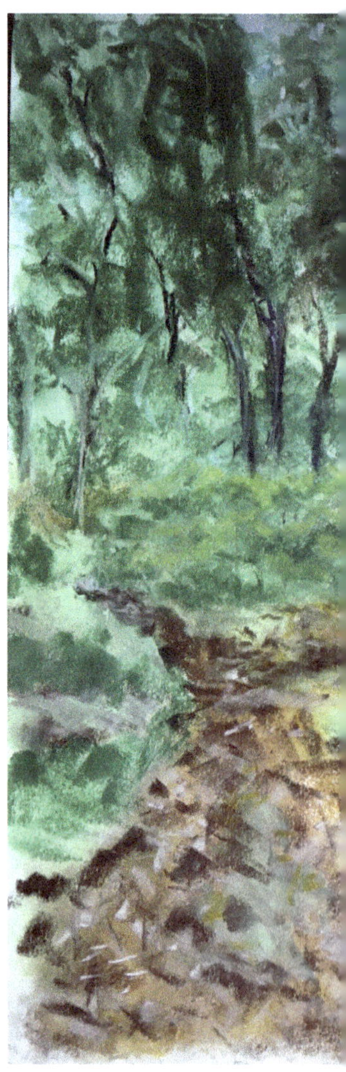

an evening calm
pervades the eucalyptus grove
historical awakening
light streaming
through laced patterns up above
shadows crossing on the path
an untimely warning
for each mortal life

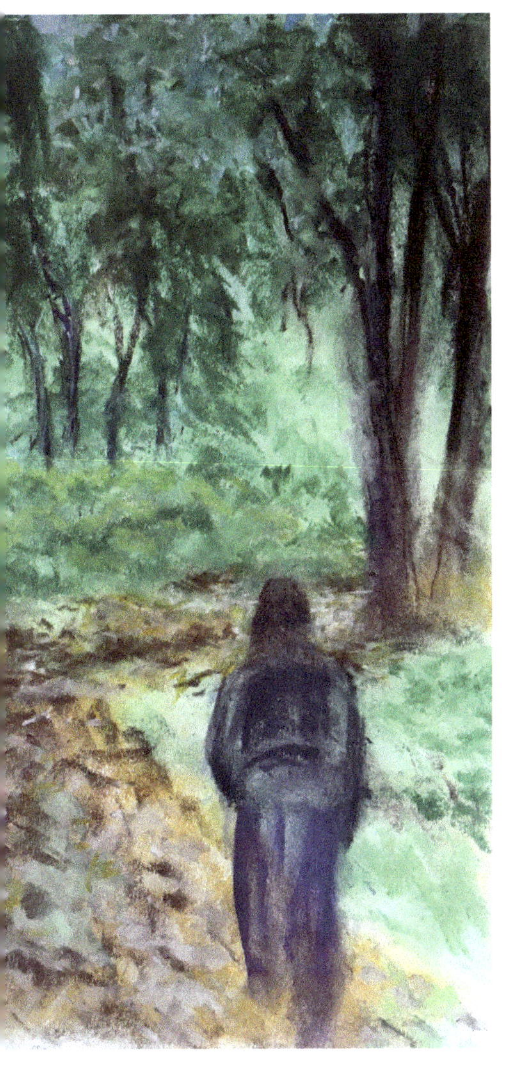

in such distant moments
the stat reports are quiet
the competing views at rest
yet belabored breathing
is heard
some where in the midst
a ventilator has come on
oxygen is needed
a nurse surrounds with care
loved ones not present,
not there

I breathe in deep and
my eyes
gaze up the eucalyptus
trunks
remembering three crosses
on the hill of calvary
in painful struggle for
their breath not coming
a cry bewailing the heavens
for a god not there

it is finished
the stat reports updated
another number is added
and the world has one
more record
of a sacred life
transcended
wrapped in a shroud
laid in a  tomb
buried in a waiting room

as the twilight
begins to merge with eucalyptus trees
and shadows overwhelm
left over thoughts
become deep felt loss
as we continue
in the struggle
to let the future manifest

Sunday morning came
no stats were needed
the rising image cast
into the aching hearts
of all afflicted
hope is found
in the will to live
upon the earth

life to

be born

and life

to come

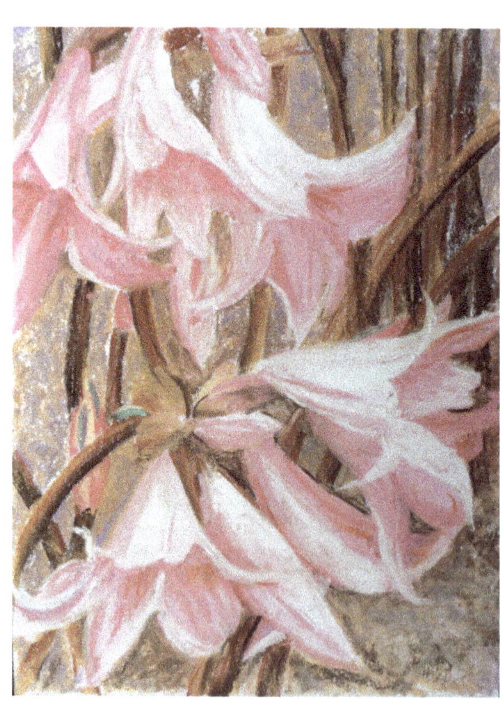

the experts and professionals say
two weeks plus of isolation
to see how and what and when something
  may occur
when symptoms come on can't smell or taste
  fever dry cough not sure if I'm safe
when symptoms become more pronounced
  hopefully tests will be available
  labs ready to diagnose
  results in time
  and procedures ready for
  those testing positive
  places ready for those testing positive
between now and when
  a vaccine is ready
  a miracle genetic response
  to fight and subdue and overcome
  the source of this virulent invasion

most of us have heard and maybe
know someone who has been contacted
or had contact with someone in some setting
and may have heard that someone has
  tragically died...

my heart goes out to their families and friends
and my thoughts bear in mind all those
who have gone into isolation
something seemingly strange to bear
estranged from the old
distanced from friends
family on hold and yet
  and yet

isolation can be something
many have sought in our history
of inner searching trying to understand
    the reasons for our misery and suffering
    ascetic attempts within a chosen place
    a time of solitude...
if you're waiting for results
if you're waiting at home a shelter in place
  make it a time of being
  by yourself

a time of delving into yourself
a cave of your own making
  out of your own instigation
a mountain top of your own climbing
  into your own memory
  and imagined future

the experts say two plus weeks
  of isolation maybe more
  history has said forty days of fasting
  maybe an exaggerated time of bodily deprivation
  maybe an exhilarating time of self transformation

my mind thinks two weeks of solitude
fourteen days and
fourteen nights being
within the thoughts
  of my existence
within the beliefs
of my birth my family my culture
my education and living experience
  the acculturated formation of my being
  coming into this time
  living on the earth...
How many books have I left on the shelves?

Have I ever remembered a sonnet? Have I ever
sat in silence and brought awareness to my breathing?
How long has it been since I've held that
  hidden tambourine or conga drum
  kept time to a song I love one that fills my heart?
let me bring them into this required isolation
  my time of
  solitude…

and when at some time a balance is wanted
to join the world wide network again
to speak and text again
to hear a loving voice the sending of heartfelt news
the live singing of songs the dancing the instant postcard
  while waiting in this limbo of transformation
    (how far can I go) when
  solitude
begets the desire to reach out and to bring in…

write a few words
  send a poem sing
a song remembered
  send a photo of your smile
    beneath your mask

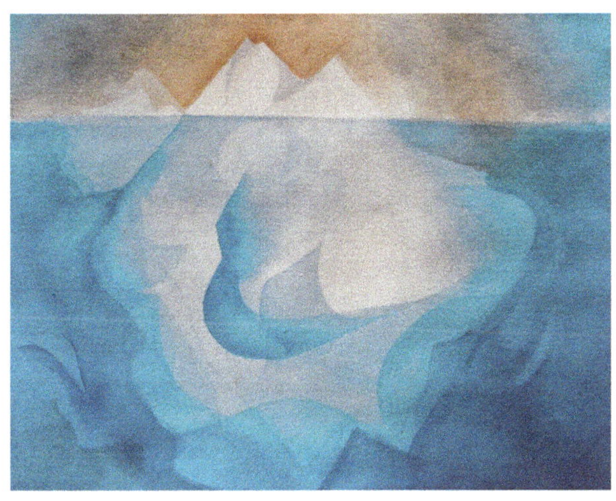

## *livestream from Bogotá*

static movement
in the remembered eye
rhythmic movement
of anticipation
tones floating
in the waiting ears
through the growing sprouting landscape
thriving in the spring of earth and sky

hills barely seen
in the mist of this rainy saturation
pampas grass now catching the ocean wind
a quick flutter back and forth
an overwhelming dracaena is also touched
its yellow green leaves flirt and flicker
titillating the birds not yet interested
while a local finch is attracted to
the butterfly bush and
the hanging beaker of food
being offered

a sultry voice
in a soft inviting
Spanish tongue
comes out of the screen propped up on the table
in the corridor of our outdoor threshold
her voice her words filling this intimate space
coming from some magical place
    in Bogotá
live from a  transformed living room
    in Bogotá
one that the world has tuned onto and into
listening to the accompanying recorded sounds
    of the DJ Bosque
and the many gathered instruments

being played when the mood
    and the feeling resonate
in their transforming of time and space…

oh the joy of the eucalyptus grove
playing swaying with the breezy blowing
of an ascending eastward wind
filled with long awaited rain
quenching the thirst of all
it touches and nurtures
after so many days of sunshine and
trembling waves upon the shore…

intentions rise out of the two figures dancing
in and out of the shadows
into the light of their instruments
into the rhythms selected and tones harmonized
creating a soundscape to play in to be in
the ethereal tones of a native American flute
    saturating the air soothing us
eyes momentarily closing
letting the sound vibrate
through our bodies emanating outward
merging into all that is growing around us

we see the soft splatter of raindrops on the deck and
    in the bird bath being filled
    for tomorrow's resurgence
these transparent droplets are holding and rolling
on the bright orange red passion flowers and
glistening among the leaves and tentacles
    slowly overtaking the old wooden fence
    that keeps no one in or out

La May offers and intones a prayer
of beauty and reverence within the natural sounds
recorded and saved in some digital memory

*Gracias Gracias Gracias*

her voice like a healing spirit fills the air
with words of solace and gratefulness and
momentary soothing in this time of such an
unknown and misunderstood invasive threat
here and for a short while time has slowed
filled us with the heart felt upwelling of
living vibrations strengthening our lives
helping us transform
the places we have come to and
the time we are in...

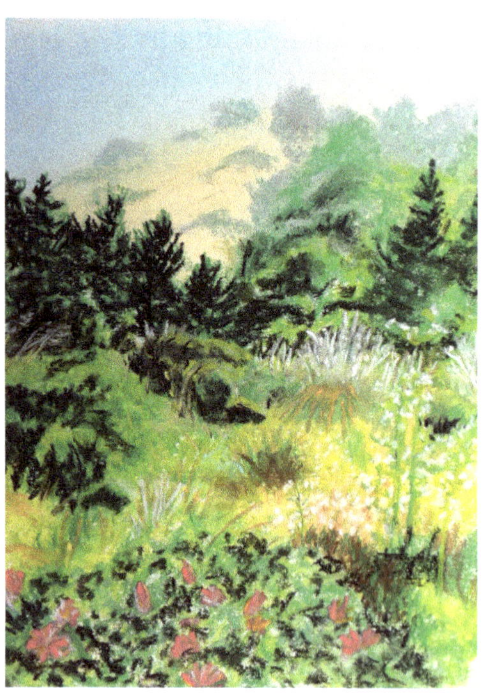

## *a hawk*

*a journey from an open deck through*
*an open wound and back again*

***afternoon stillness***
***hawk sits on a wavering branch***
***a mouse in the grass***

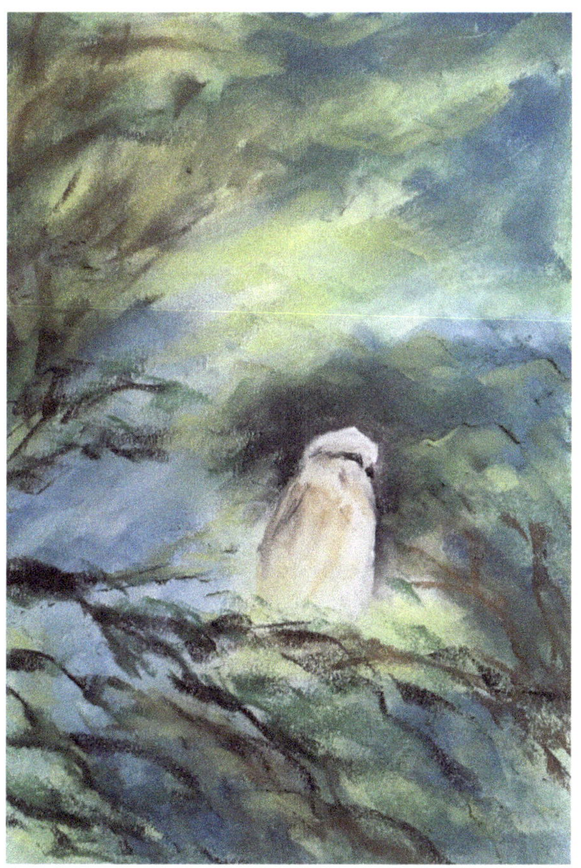

**I'm out back**
**on deck**
**blue sky**
**so blue**
**passion flowers so orange red**

who is that tweeting in the grandfather tree
    a white crowned sparrow
    waiting for an answer
    in the left over wild behind our garden

a hawk is noticed
on a wavering branch
sitting looking into the stillness
surveying the grass the ground for any movement
daily hunger felt, the search is on
    for a gopher eating the roots of the radish
    the kale plant before its grown
    aphids are on the leaves or are they
    bees on the blue rosemary flowers

a hawk is waiting
looking
another day
of being under
the contrails of a 747 super sonic jet
rising out of San Francisco airport
a mechanical miracle still flying
in these times
    who is still flying
    who is moving in place
    who is still sitting in a row
    we remember
do you remember Afghanistan Vietnam
   I remember
our flight to Istanbul landing on the first day
    of an incredible new airport
no one there
a huge cavern of modernity
a structural miracle
a church by another name
    from a place of prayer and transformation

to a place of transportation
ordained in economic belief
the call to prayer is now a call for departures
to other vast worshipping spaces
of physical destinations
security found duty free moments
faithful anticipation of an in bound traveler

now comes the sound of a one-engined plane
overhead circling towards Half Moon Bay airport
just off the coast
runways are between Highway One and a bluff
with hilltop hiking trails and historic footprints
of the once thriving indigenous people
and Portola's horses once looking over
that waving splashing sparkling Pacific
so close to their "discovery" of that Ohlone bay
soon to be named after Saint Francis

a hawk
with stern eyes
stern demeanor
furtive glances
bushy tan feathers
looking full fed
but still looking
while kamikaze humming birds buzz by
flittering and fluttering
all around it
is this what it means
to be still
to be content
to be one with all one needs
to be in the moment
of a raptor's awareness

it seems I've just played with
    the idea...

but an insistent tweet tweet tweet
keeps repeating like someone else
I've come to know
   through the news the videos
   exacerbating the issues with
   advisors rolling their eyes
and with a persistent disregard and
   disrespect for those wanting some truth
   and civilized response

somewhere near here
there is a softer response
a singing tweet has provoked a
bay bay bay bay of recognition
a possible meeting or a tryst of sorts

I hear a click of wings
an aggressive humming bird has taken over
and chased off a ruby red beauty
its long beak goes in to a red plastic flower
the look up
the scorn of keep away

not so many years ago
John Muir heard the call of the
mountains again and felt the mist of Yosemite Falls
and brought back the beauty and stories
    to his valley home
infusing the curious minds and hearts to come
I am fortunate enough to
sit with a hawk
a wild distance away
no directive from the governor

just an understanding of
risk and distance and wild beauty

ahh but a fluttering yellow brown butterfly
has found the golden lilies
and joined our late afternoon happy hour
our sweet inhaling and imbibing twilight time

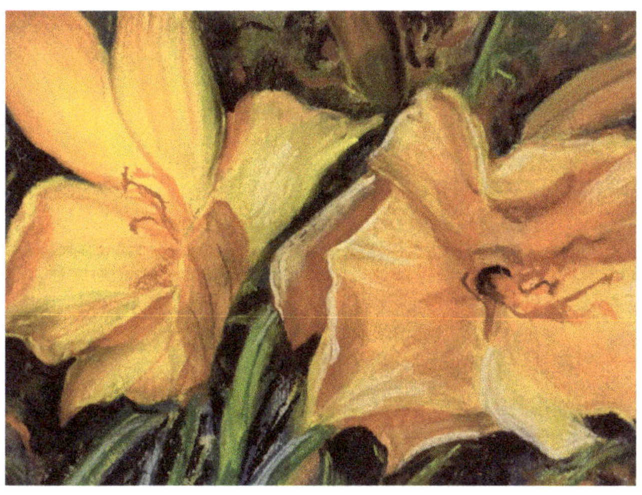

to have lived this long
to have opened my mind
to this wavering flowing
flying flapping fantastic sometimes
    very still world

listen
I am overcome with
being alive
in such a moment
no internet needed
    the GPS is not the territory

how do the hours
pass for a hawk
on a branch of green
quietly blinking and waiting
for the slightest movement
    like my potential blank paper
    waiting to be filled with
remembered sunlight breaking
through darkening clouds
this hawk is hoping to see a meal
    move in the grass and yes
we begin to get antsy too
even hungry fortunately
our meal is in the refrigerator
waiting to be fried

and still a hawk is there
and I have come closer
to stillness in its presence
like a quote from Ram Dass
    *"the quieter you become*
    *the more you can hear"*
like a moment of being in the world
    and yet being in the constant in between
    of knowing and not knowing
a strange state of mind
that has arrived and affected our lives
being in the now of a virulent virus
    an unseen invasion attaching
    itself to our breath of life

and now and again being in the throes
    of discontent
    in the streets of masked faces anonymous
    batons face shields tear gas coughing
    a flashpoint of injustice recognized

a knee pressing on the breath of life
videos viewed world wide
seen again and again
stirring a cauldron of protests
and kneeling and commentary
under a sky of such blue clarity
and a field of green verdant life
strange paradoxes and ripening fruit
growing within the zeitgeist of our times...

be here now
has become ironically real
we know the past
we are not sure of the future
we live in the risk and the upheaval and
the momentary joy
of the present

sing it Jimmy
*"the world is upside down*
*the world is turning around"*

a hawk is still here on a branch
no nesting in place
free to fly
free to be

I am
in the stillness
as free as I can be in the world
within the buzzing clicking flitting of life
and the awareness and resilience and time
of struggle for change

watching a humming bird syphoning
from the red plastic flower
filled with sugar water

I am
still growing and being
    in the waves of the earth
    in the waves of the air
    in the remembrance of the constant surf
    and a primal world not too far from here...

is the hawk still there
    no
the hawk has flown
the glass is empty
the sun is setting
tis eventide
    my heart beats on

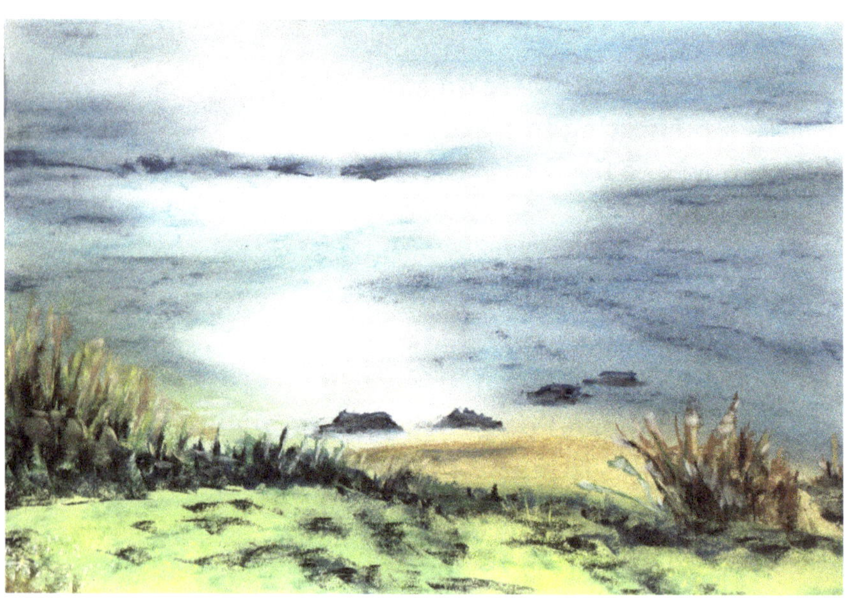

the heart starts to pump
the spirit begins to fly
I've heard the reasons
I've lived with the reasons
  got my mask and stayed the distance
but I've got that feeling
  that keeps percolating up
  how long can I be should I be
  contained bottled up isolated
    within these walls
    within my thoughts...

so I've thrown some caution to the wind
  some risk into the stats
hopefully not a burden or a threat to anyone else
  that I might drive past
I'm traveling on highway one
driving south…
like that long ago song

*"traveling on highway one*
*feeling the warmth of the sun*
*no matter where you've been*
*no matter what you've done*
*you'll feel like you have just begun*
*traveling on highway one…"*

almost to San Gregorio Beach
I know it's closed
so I make a left instead
higher up pull over park
onto the old Stage Road

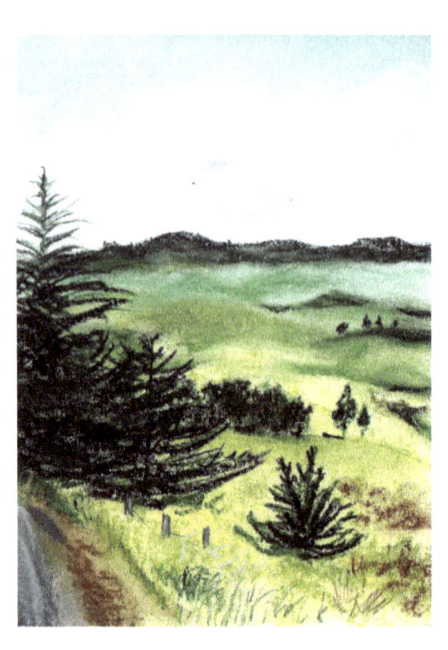

overlooking the valley and
that country highway
meandering east
going through and surrounded
by the green hills and
wavy grass
with a coastal breeze
so refreshing
breathe deep
sitting in the van settling in
on the hill with a view
the windows down and a
cup of coffee too

who has been here before
who has heard the birds
with such vibrato
sing out of the many generations
that have come and gone

who has walked this luscious valley
who has walked it by themselves
who has walked this verdant valley
who has lived it loved it explored it
and at some time demarcated it
and raised their cows and children on it
who has felt its seasons of living and dying
and witnessed this spring time of renewal
on the land and in themselves

and who has wandered on the beach
of this coast so near so close
the one with thousands of footprints
once implanted in the sand and lost over the ages
washed away with the incessant surf and
the in and out flowing of the waves and tide

we too had our time
our moment on that beach
not so many years ago
yet a lifetime ago
three graces stood up
at an annual gathering
three women surrounded by
    spouses and friends
three women told their story
    of miraculous discovery
three women beamed in joy and
    spoke of children to come

Saint Gregory looked in and heard
the news and the sky opened up
and the surf clapped in raucous response

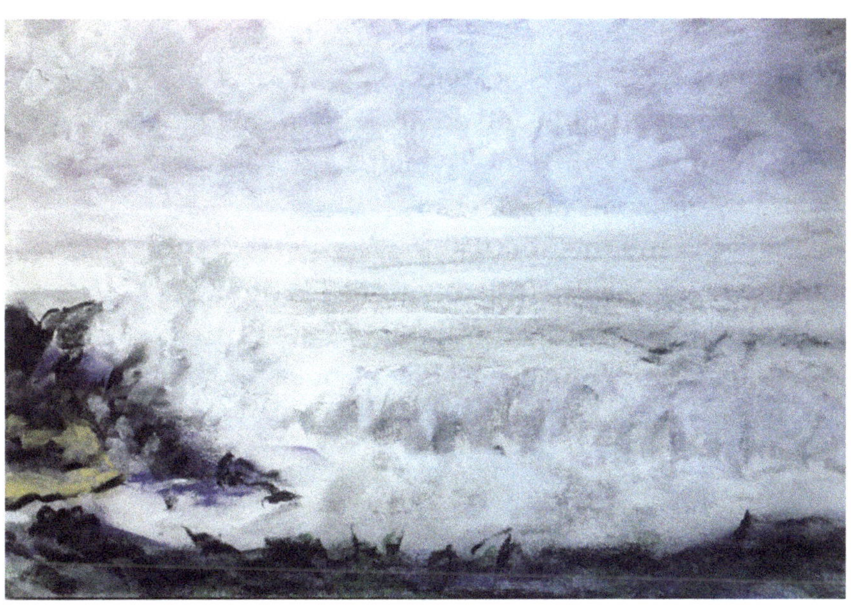

this old Stage Road turns and goes down
from my point of view my surveillance
of this abundant land winding down
to the intersection of that highway
to La Honda and Alice's Restaurant and more

but here now on the right is the General Store
I don't know if I can go in or if
it's even open I'm not sure but
I'll stop and take a look too bad
I was unfortunately right...
    *not open until May*
good to know someone is still running it
and someday soon it will open again
a veritable institution down here on the coast
    with an old stand up bar
    the likes of which you can't find anymore

however inside you'll find the odd postcard and
the oversized Levis on the wall and a
welcoming table of books you can't pass by
    all with an attitude and something to say
    be it thoughts philosophy history
    and the spirit of our day
on the weekend the joint is bursting
and the few tables are filled with heads bobbing
to the sounds of a local group that fit the bill
they know their songs well they've been
singing them since Ken Kesey lived in La Honda
and the world was ripe for outrageous possibility
    well now
the prankster spirit still remains
    in the joy of their songs letting the guitar picking
    span the years while we tap the floor and
    some sing along...

and the times did go by
with many a dog on the beach
and youngsters running free
in and out of the waves building forts
with the yearly harvest of drift wood
the left over jetsam and flotsam from the storms
and the strange life on and in this place
    this land sea and sky…

Now I'm traveling north on highway one
the evening's come and I'm almost done
another song has come to mind

*"country road take me home*
*to the place I've come to know*
*El Granada coastal haven*
*take me home country road…"*

my heart has eased
my spirit has flown
I've taken a chance
    thrown this afternoon's euphoria into the mix
    and my soul into a poem that might be read…
so hopefully I've not been a burden or a threat
    to anyone else
in these times of concern and giving and loving
in all the ways we know how
all the ways we can anticipate

    and yes
    still we live…

*sometimes I question words that abstract the real*
*can they ever take the place of tragic loss and pain*
*we hear we see we feel we live with the horrors*
*that go deep into our memory our brain…*
*still I speak and sing within this existential state*
*and write the words that may somehow*
*nourish and resonate…*

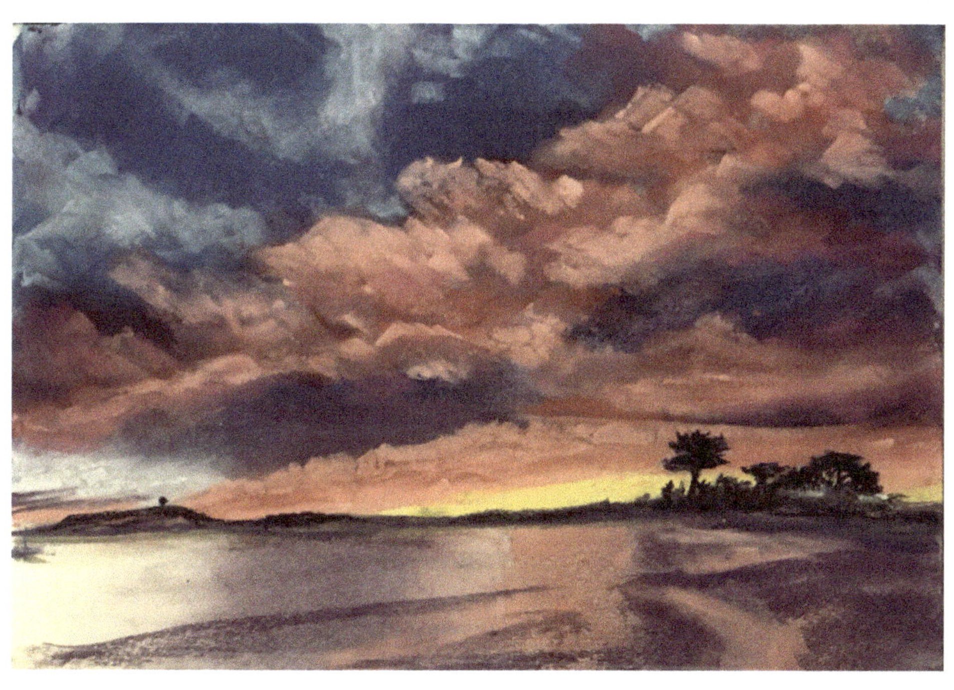

## *beating hearts*

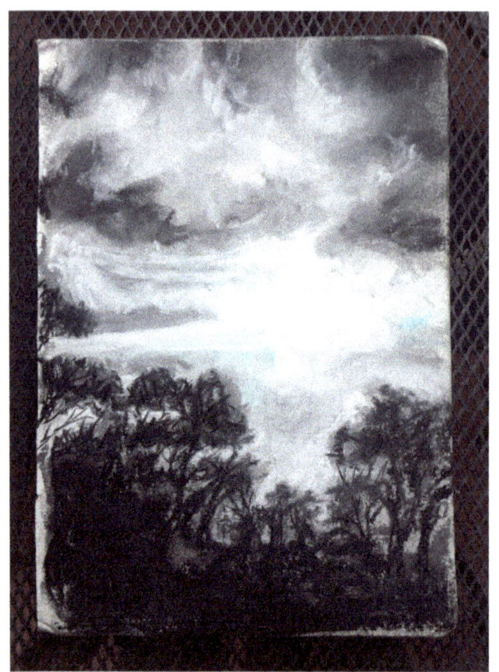

I was out of touch
when I heard the news
a violent act
chaos and shots
the distance that
the bullets crossed
when a calculating demon
fired
into the beating hearts of
Las Vegas

the gates had opened
tickets taken
bags were searched
in anticipation
a secure feeling
the ground unshaken
when a calculating demon fired
into the beating hearts of Las Vegas

in all innocence
the fans had come
from an open stage
the songs were sung
stars were shining
movement begun
when the calculating demon fired
into the beating hearts of Las Vegas

was it desperation
or disconnect
from human feeling
that makes a suspect
finger the weapons

aim and discharge
become a calculating demon firing
into the beating hearts of Las Vegas

the human flesh
was ripped and torn
in shock and pain
the unforeseen
blood spurting
on the village green
as the calculating demon fired
into the beating hearts of Las Vegas

what takes over
the rabid mind
breaking the covenant
of human kind
faceless murder
abstract sum
as the calculating demon fired
into the beating hearts becoming numb

what is tomorrow
in such warped brains
born in a culture
where suicide remains
what of the daughter
the son born to give
as the calculating demon fired
into the beating hearts that we have outlived

as minds and weapons have fired
into the beating hearts of us all

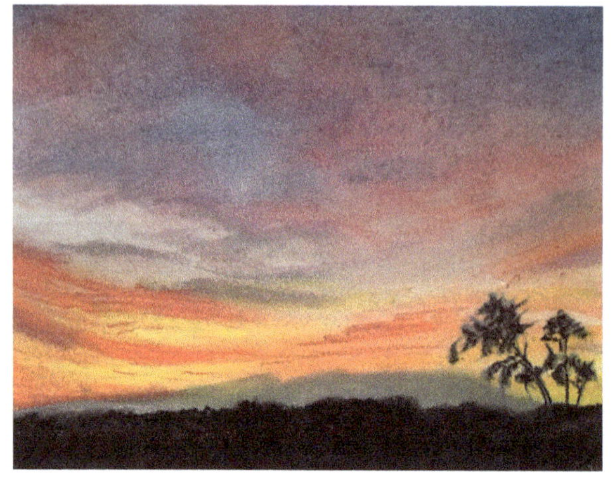

## *the flames*

the flames they
came to Paradise
they came in fury
in senseless rage
with no seventh
day to rest in this
time and age

they came to burn
what had been born
in the womb of a valley and hills
in the midst of forest offerings
    trees cut down for
    shelters fields paths and roads
    the warmth of fires in a fireplace
now the road is filled with fear
desperation between the flames and belching smoke
    past blackened stumps
    and remnants of foundations
        left with nothing now
    no more shade no more branches
    for the resting of wings or
    the buds of spring and leaves

they came to burn
what had been built
with nails driven into wood and shingles
with every roof beam raised
    by every hand taught the craft
    throughout the yesterdays
now left with nails strewn in the ash
        left with nothing now

contorted metal resting in the ground
they came to burn
who had been born
in a mother's pain and joyful touch
becoming growing singing
    holding hot chocolate in a cup
    around the warmth of stones and a fireplace fire
        left with nothing now
only blackened remnants still standing
amidst the ruins of kitchens and beds and
love once known

they came to burn
those who have grown old
who left their foot prints
on the steps and garden paths
    who talked and greeted
    neighbors well known and loved
    who knew where the children played
    and drank a hot toddy by the fireplace fire
who saw no way out
    smothered by smoke epitome of horror
without goodbyes or the
touch of a hand

they came to burn
what had permeated and infused
every corner of every loving living room
every chair and bed and book
every moment lived with a family or alone
every moment lived in secure forevers and
thoughts of tomorrow
    left only with what was once here
    and there and known

the flames they came to Paradise
they came in fury
in pent up rage
with no seventh day to rest in this time and age

they came to burn
what had withstood the years
now just blackened stumps remained
around the cement and rebar devastation
    once a communal place
    once a general store
    hardware feed and groceries
    a local coffee house
   with a fire in the fireplace
now overtaken by hellish flames and
    belching blinding smoke
who has died and who has not been found
in this community burned to the ground
they came to burn
those who dared to subdue the flaming wrath
who dared to raise their swords
against the fire breathing beings bursting from within
those who risked their lives
true heroes out of myths and prisons
silhouetted against the hellish firelight
listening for the anguished voice
the desperate man woman child
in the race for life
    trying to contain stop and stem
    the conflagration
   however whatever way they could

the flames they came to Paradise
they came in fury
in pent up rage
with no seventh day to rest in this time and age

they came to burn
and send their ash
into a sky once filled with dreams
and daily occurrences
to send their particulates
into the atmosphere
and the breath of millions
floating and remaining with masks on and off
  while the sun turned an intense fiery red
  rupturing the smoke filled day
for photos and images as yet unnamed

no words will ever soothe the pain
the grief that comes again and again
it's just our thoughts that let us dwell
on those who are going through
  this fire this hell

and yet I feel a thrust
a gut level heart felt need
to write some words
that make their way through
the flames and smoke
the layers of ash
the grief and loss
heartache and pain

for all the things we can
and cannot do

yes the flames they came to paradise
they came in fury
in pent up rage
with no seventh day to rest in this time and age

spirals of fury eddies of worry
the atmosphere is acting up warming seas
hot air turbulence desert winds
circling around the earth
hurricane force tornados off course
god or nature what's for sure water levels rising
opportunities found water levels rising
exploitation unbound water levels rising

yet we go on with our routines
and live on in our habitual dreams
projected on our virtual screens
away from the direction of actual scenes

there may be an abstract connection somehow somewhere
as events fill us in interrupt us detract us while
algorithms sift through what is true somehow
becoming fake and faulty news with raging ranting views
angry men and women holding onto
what they feel they know and emotionally show
what has been historically seen in their
struggle to survive to stay secure in the
traditions and beliefs they have known
those circumstantial chances of being born and
dropped and held in some place upon this earth

spiral of words apathetic tweets
"thugs and rapists" coming down the streets
while privileges abound and deals are hidden
venal approval has now been given
talking hate screeching birds fake truth rising
integrity lost what is the cost fake truth rising
go with your gut get out of their rut fake truth rising

but we go on with our routines
and live on in our habitual dreams
projected on our virtual screens
away from the direction of actual scenes

spirals of loss forgetting the cost
while some live in luxury
with all kinds of security
no gated community
or subdivision conformity
can stop the hurricanes from blowing
    stop the lethal ashes from choking
    stop the rivers from drying
while some dams are overflowing
money can only buy so much
pensions and income those will be done
acres of fires hard times rising
earth's funeral pyres hard times rising
desperate grasp for the past hard times rising

yet we go on with our routines
and live on in our habitual dreams
projected on our virtual screens
away from the realization of actual scenes

can we still find ways that make sense
travel on paths of reason and rationality
hold out and offer an olive branch
before retaliation rears its irrational head
light just one more light
in the shadows of our desperation
shine just one more light
before the last minute of deadly decisions
Turn on one more light

before we go on with our routines
and live on in our habitual dreams
projected on our virtual screens
away from the realization of actual scenes

spirals of plenty in this century
    let redistribution abound
let us go forward let go act out spread around
life saving resources and recognition
    out of the hollows and shadows of our concerns
hold out our hand to someone next door
    down the street over a border
find some kernels of compassion
    for a knocked down fallen down brother sister
find some balm some opportunity
    for those who struggle in a wasteland
        not necessarily of their own making

before we are all dragged out by the riptides
of our accumulated and irreversible actions
before we are all numbers and faces
seen in the data of profiled abstractions
before we are all overcome by the avalanches
of destruction and ecological devastation
before we all face a pandemic raging
through our social and economic existence

can we still make a break out of our routines
live in the potential of our dreams
utilize and vitalize our resourceful means
can we retake remake reclaim a stake in our

living breathing future scenes?

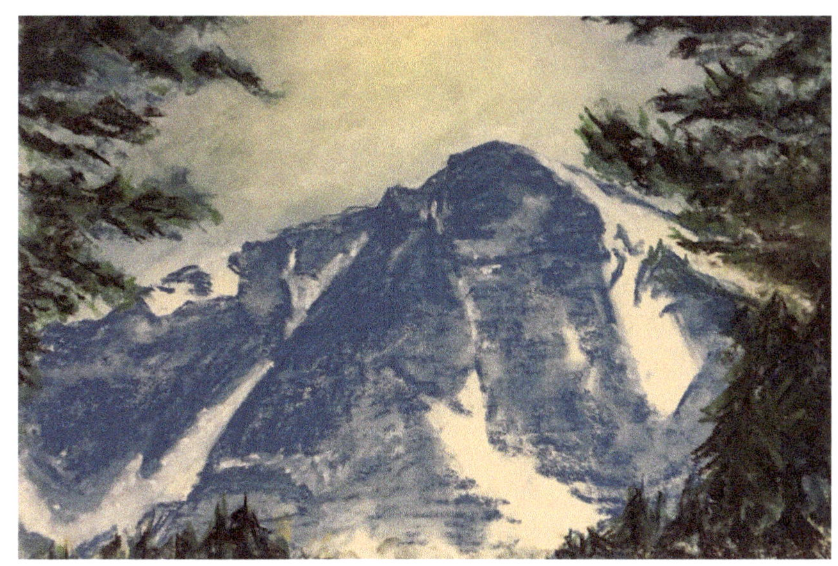

## *day of solitude*

day of solitude
  a novel of sorts
    leaning back with
  sunlight on the firs and pines reaching for the sky
      pointed green needles swooping down
      all swaying in the afternoon wind
      as it dives down and caresses
      the face of Mt Tallac
hold on
  do not descend
    oh blessed giver and traveler of light
      do not allow
this earth to turn into shades of gray
and coming darkness
with a flowing stream the only left over constancy
rushing in the midst of random sounds
  rushing through the belly of the primal
    dying growing and renewing life and ground

day of solitude
an evening of sorts
leaning back with the
shadows on variegated pines reaching for the sky
with pointed needles shown as silhouettes
all turning in the twilight wind
still diving down and caressing
the face of Mt Tallac

it is late
your descent is inevitable
oh blessed giver and traveler of light
you have allowed
this earth to turn into shades of gray
and emanent darkness
with a flowing stream the only left over constancy
rushing in the midst of random sounds
rushing through the belly of the primal
dying growing and renewing life and ground

day of solitude
a turning of sorts
leaning back with the
stars illuminating the darkened path
pointed needles vaguely outlined
stillness pervading becoming
the inner breath that once caressed
the face of Mt Tallac

we can change
the game can wait
somewhere in the recesses of addiction
somewhere in the bucking
  of the odds
somewhere in the enticement
  of temptation there is
a voice of overcoming
  a focus a meaning

we can change
the killer can wait
somewhere in the affliction
  of pain
somewhere in the brutalizing
  of another
somewhere in the humiliation
  of the weakest
is the sanctity of life
  a recognition an awareness

we can change
the beast can wait
somewhere in the depths
  of primal urges
somewhere in the latent rising
  of desire
somewhere in the thrusting
  of forces
is a remembrance of beauty
  a touch a first kiss
we can change we can become….

# *somewhere*

somewhere in some
small cafe
over iced lemon and Dubonnet
sitting in anticipation
searching in each other's eyes
hearing one another's voice
some words meant
some words soft
stories started
smiles acknowledged

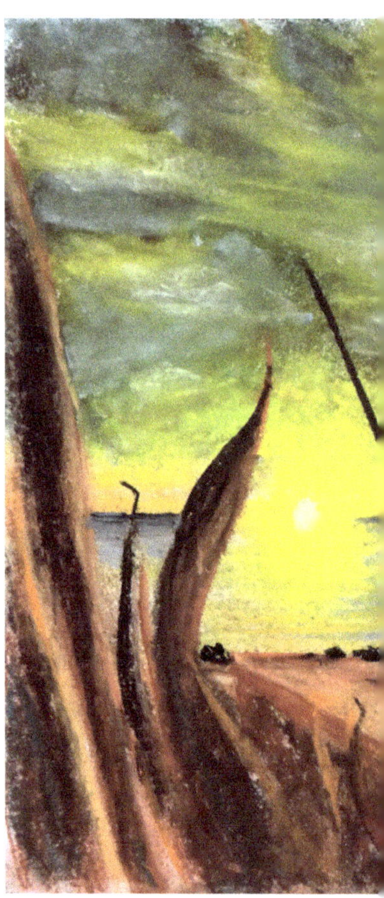

somewhere on some
high bar stool
with an Irish coffee to refuel
sitting in contemplation
searching the heart left by itself
hearing a singer's song
some words caught
some remembered
when life started
not yet departed

somewhere in some
forgotten alley
hands are shaking a deal is made
sitting in anticipation
broken lives find a moment
in a flawed communion
some touch needed
some satisfied
life rewarded
death averted

somewhere in some
strobe lit place
bodies moving with a reggae beat
faces dark and then elated
searching for a counter part
one lost with an open heart
someone gone
someone here
a space unfulfilled
love deterred

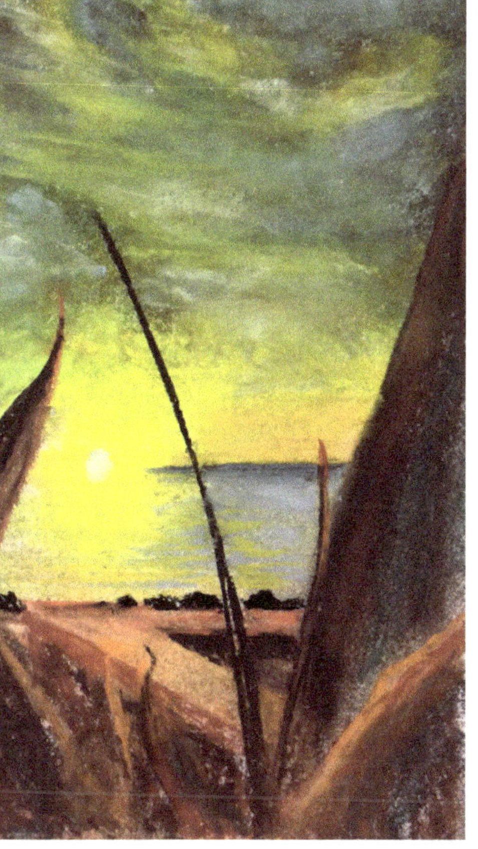

somewhere in some
art gallery
off the street by the sea
looking for revelation
searching
for some iconic view
transcending images
in light
some quickly fade
some reach deep
what's remembered
life confirmed
in my sight

for the sake of family and friends
finding ourselves together
finding ourselves in this time on this day

with the knowledge
of human tragedy near by
with every smoke filled horizon
with every breath we've taken

can we be there now
take a moment
be mindful
bring our thoughts and our hearts to

those who have lost
a loved one
in the smoke and flames
still being searched for
in the remains
a charred bone
a cell phone
a ring
strewn among the ashes

is it then that someone grasps
a hand reaching out of desperation

suddenly we are faced with
nature's indifference and human failings
a telephone pole falling sparking
dry grass a branch flames bursting
convergences so tragic and so dire

is it then that small miracles whisper
and question our thoughts of despair

and yet we are reminded of
nature's caprice and human jeopardy
hurricanes raising roofs uprooting trees
unstoppable destruction and death
children's voices crying so hard to bear

is it then that streams of light
come through a broken window

do we need to be reminded
of our extended communities those
coming into our lives our neighborhoods
    with eyes of hesitation
    reactions to strangers
who have similar aspirations
who also struggle and work to build a future

is it then that a blanket is offered
a basket of bread at the right time

do we still need to be reminded
that parables have been told morality taught
rising out of too many tragic acts with
social contracts broken and now multiplied
in our internet of callous commentary

is it then that we need to look into a mirror
look into ourselves see what we have sown

and let dormant seeds break through the darkness
reach for the light sprouting and flowering
spoken words read repeated and offered again

*"treat others as you would have them treat you"*

for the sake of family and friends
finding ourselves together
finding ourselves here in this time in this age
of vulnerability and impermanence
being inundated and inoculated by
sounds and images repeated senses assaulted
from every hand held media connection

is it then that words of uncovered truth
must be spoken and rise above fear?

can we be here now
take a moment
be mindful
bring our thoughts and our selves into
a quiet introspection
that touches the deeper aspects of who we are
   can we find meaning in a gesture a touch
   can we find gratitude right next to us
   can we find ourselves in our differences

for the sake of family and friends
finding ourselves together
finding ourselves in this time on this day

is it now that
we can raise
our head and
look up and
pursue small
acts of love?

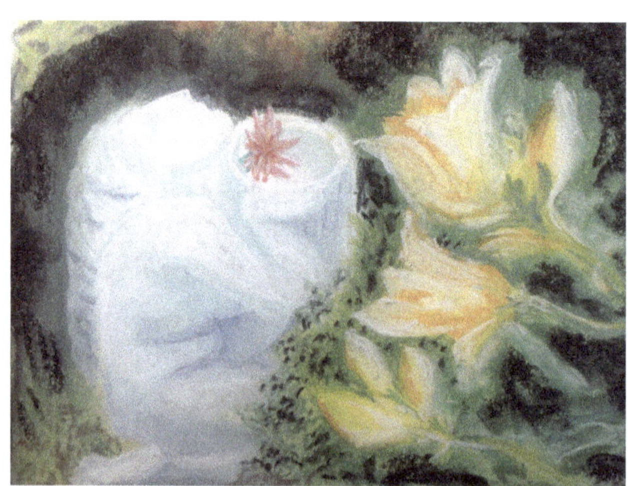

## *contradictions*

in the wonder of a morning sunrise

nature's news is waiting for us
*with no internet connection in the air*

when rays of light silhouette the trees
and memory brings back ancient times

nature's news is open to becoming
*with no internet connection to be found*

transcendent thoughts emerge stream out
amongst the rising columns of variegated bark
rooted in the cycle of dying decaying and rebirth

nature's news is all within the ground
*with no internet connection to be made*

with a notebook of pages ready to fill
up the hillside with assorted ideas
a hammock strapped between two giants
allows the mind the body to grow still

nature's news is to be taken in
*with no internet connection coming on*

in the dappled beauty of this forest moment
a murmuring stream comes out of silence
a slight breeze moves the upper branches
a song is repeated by an unknown bird
while aspen leaves shake and softly rustle

nature's news is there to be heard
*with no internet connection to the sound*

in this fulfilled space of earthly turning
on a soft and giving pine needle path
near rock and manzanita settings
in the twilight of this occasion
the sun is slowly disappearing
behind a mountain and resplendent lake

nature's news is there to be seen
*with no internet connection to overcome*

walking back to our man made home
built over the centuries hand to hand
slowly the axe the hammer the level
the square and compass were carried
from one sacred structure to another
from one village to every river setting
until our stories infused the wood and stone

nature's news is there to be discovered
*with no internet connection at this time*

on a heady road trip over Carson Pass
history fills the spaces in between
the tree line and the granite quartz
wagons were pulled and lowered
before the highways rounded curves
until a stagecoach ride on rutted roads
brought the high Sierras into view
a vista both majestic and heart pounding

nature's news is everywhere to be felt
*with no internet connection to the world*

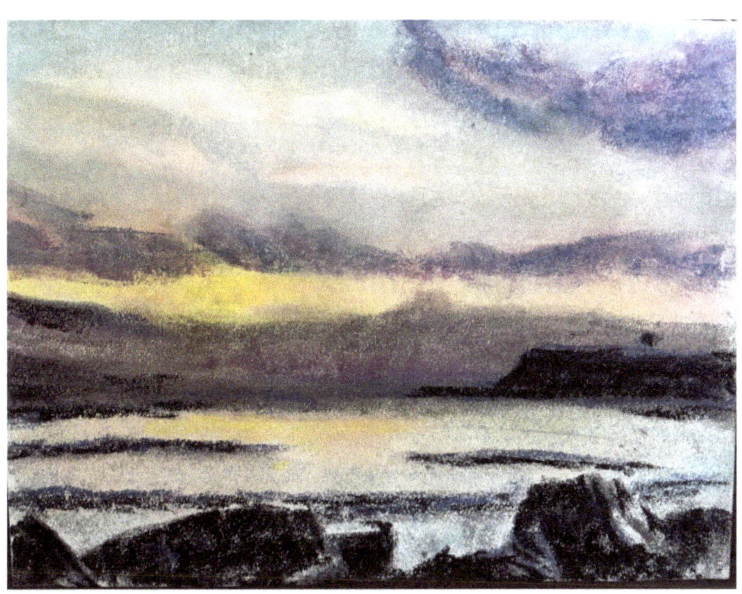

to begin again
to continue
to begin
to live with the essence of life again
to sip a martini on the deck of possibilities
to laugh
to feel the coastal breeze waft around my ears
my hair
sitting on a cushioned chair
to hear the unknown birds sing
and start again
in the memory of Leonard Cohen's words
rising from desire to his final testament
to write a few verses for Toothless Floyd
Clifford's friend living on a farm in Indiana
while the afternoon passes at the Ebbtide Cafe
to say guten tag to the impresario Harpo
to see the glistening waters of the bay
on a sunlit day

to begin again
to continue to hear a seal barking in Pillar Point harbor
in the jetty safe harbor for the fishing boats
bringing back the salmon and the crab
after early morning beginnings
at the Press coffee cafe
to the overcast cloud cover gently
but inexorably coming between the blue heaven
and the green rain soaked hills in my sight
to the butterfly bush waiting and the passion vine
growing the seeds of their lily like flowers
and the cypress trees waving to the sound
of a small plane attempting to land at the HMB airport
knowing the overcast covering will be penetrated
effortlessly within a remembered landing
to begin again
to see the lime green sea change randomly
with the movement of the clouds
to a blue green shade again
to hear the breaking waves constantly
come in rhythmic movements
to see the white washed patterns of foam
flowing back out and sinking
in the crunching and rumbling of the next wave
to remember an older cultural wave of poetics break
into the Ebbtide by that veritable barista Clifford
    with a copy of *"Violent Milk"* published in 1983
immersed and churning in the San Francisco scene
of post beat poets reconstructing the language
until every word had its own context
    displayed on the page
read by itself or read together
spoken in abstraction and singularity
to a future that is now still living thriving
the *"exquisite corpse"* in the minds of all
that our experiential past can ascertain

an ocean of consciousness
a stream of consciousness
to peruse in a surreal state of being

to begin again
after a night's descent into the abyss
in an excruciating and life questioning state
the tearing of the web of illusory order
  that we weave together
throughout every aspect of our existence
to be in the throes and midst of life giving
  birth and circumstance
that invokes the falling of a card
knowing that the dealer holds the cards
in the order that has been shuffled and ordained
not by godly decree but by an order of uncertainty
with established values and values of placement
from least powerful to the most powerful
to wait and wait again
for the next card the final card
  in this particular microcosm

like a "Match Point" in Woody's film
where the ball stops on top of the net and
everything in the world is poised
for its movement backward or forward
a movement determined by chance or the stars
waiting for a moment in our lives again
within the extensions we have created
through interactions and games of chance
agreed upon or not agreed upon by the players
  and strategies like that

to begin again
to continue
to begin
to live into a new morning
after a sleepless nightmare night
to have the birds sing again

and let stronger habits be realized
overcoming the momentary
immersion into the far reaches
of another universe
to get up and get the body moving
out of bed out of the house
on the bike
towards the rising sun

  to begin again
    to begin again

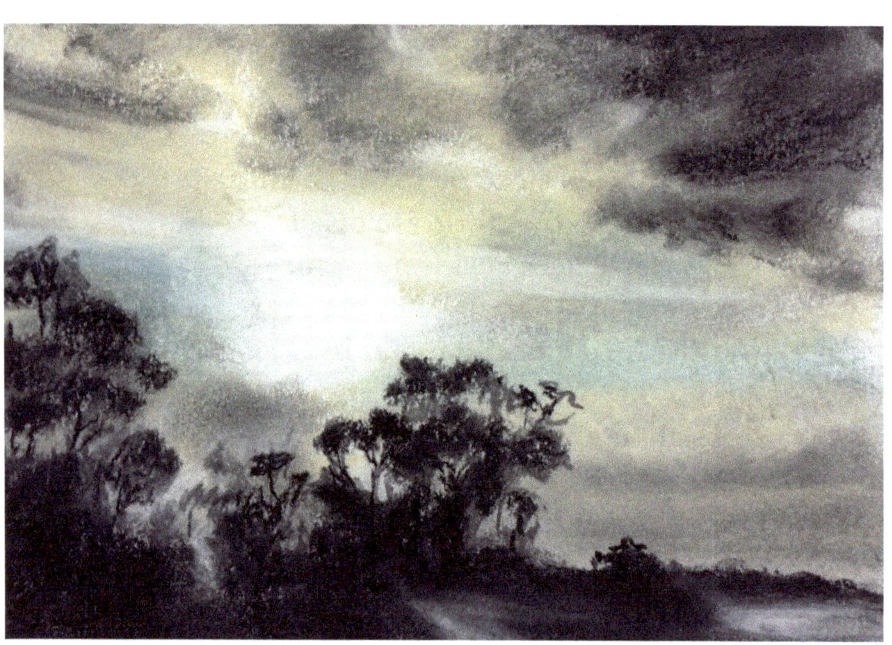

in the depths of my being
inside the hollow of my soul
  whatever soul is or is not
  what ever essence there is or is not
something ultimately inexplicable
something beating like the heart
something pulsing in the body
out and in the depths of awareness
something emerging and sensed
something boring into the basis
of all life force and life blood…

within the physical dividing of cells
the orbiting of electrons
the splitting of the nucleus
the center that does not hold
in the black of a black hole

   and yet and yet
as if by the impulse of one rising star
one shining beam of light
miracles emerge
as laughter and tears
as poems and songs
and images of our created world
as seeds of ideas and ideals of our striving
as dreams and myths and magic
out of age old desires
out of the ferment of creation
   and resilience

*it's a new democracy*
*so new that we can try to imagine*
*it's a love of freedom*
*that rises out of who we are*

*who we can still*
*remember to be...*

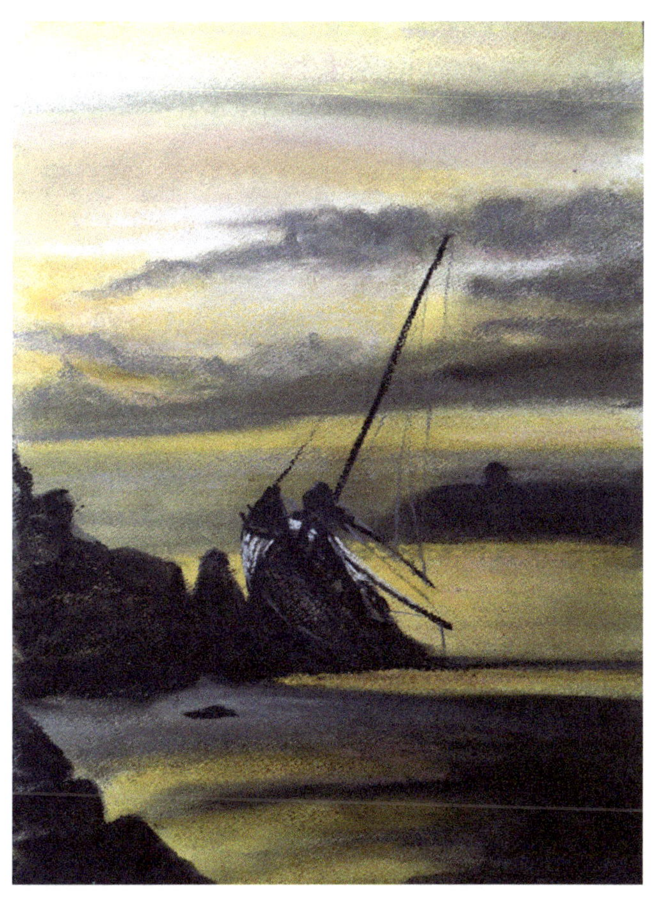

## *a voice*

a candle ready to be lit
the piled up lit ready to be read
ideas ready
to be taken in
thought about mulled over
slept with dreamed on
oh the inner world
becoming real being born
emerging
out of the chrysalis of transformation
becoming the work
on a page a screen
words spoken and sung
a voice ready to be heard

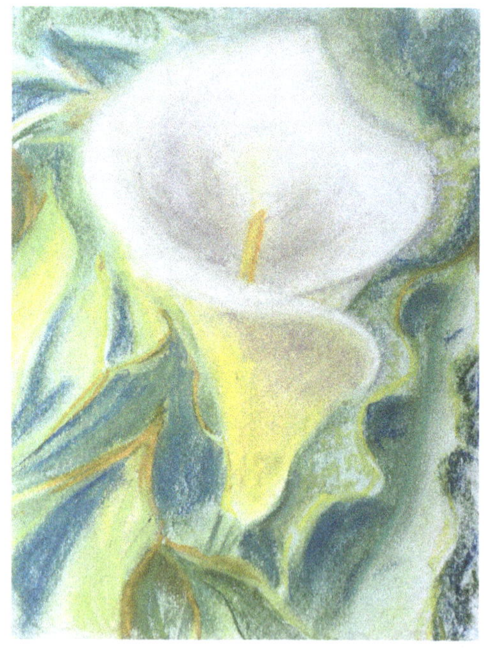

on the borders
of abstraction
lines drawn upon the earth
fought over killed over defended and agreed upon
demarcations of circumstance
that history won't let go
all earthly life fills the spaces in between
humanity must pay heed to the barbed wire
the walls the lines at the airports
where the incased authorities decide
if the passports match
and the dogs sniff
and the guns are heavy and obvious

on the borders
of desperation
walking running
riding the buses
jumping onto a boxcar
the open pickup trucks
the closed semi trucks
holding on to every breath
holding a child's body
the hand of a daughter
the arm of a son
children born in a mother's pain
suckled and nourished
within a mother's love
a father nearby and in the world
not of his own making but of his working
hands rough from the fields and too long the days
fighting for fairness too often denied
too often brutally denied

in a village somewhere in a country
far from the prying eyes of decency
with no recourse to justice
men women in uniforms
local militias state armies
not obvious in a dim light
following orders of an unseen authority
following orders amid claims of innocence
following orders once decided by world courts
as crimes against humanity
too often deaths of innocents mothers fathers
perpetrated centuries ago and just yesterday

in a village somewhere in a valley
families live in the rhythms of their traditions
and in the transitions to the modern incursions
the on going massage of cultures
they live in their daily needs of water and food
live in the arts of their ancestors
and the lore of their natural surroundings
live in their communion their moments of love
joined by millions around the world
on a street somewhere near a home
growing fearful of the local predators
organized gangs of young people with few options
the sound of gunfire
the tap of boots on gravel local militias
the click of ammunition in the chamber military orders
the rap at the door
a father is taken fighting for a plot of land
wanted by anonymous greed and disconnected
politicos and board room decision makers

a daughter is raped by a misguided uniformed man
a mother is abused by the anger of a frustrated
husband with no where to turn
leaving fear and foreboding
in the wake of their exploitation and abuse
destroying the connections of family
community all the work for a better life
and a hopeful future

within gnawing fears somewhere in a fragile home
a mother packs what she can
what she may need
to keep her children alive
on an unknown journey
leaving everything she's known
leaving her past her familiar life
her spoons her pots her rugs woven
in a corner of their room
her children's clothes and toys
all they've ever known

on a bus somewhere in a strange land
going north with a suitcase with
a few pesos saved over the years
holding her daughter close
her son asleep beside her
late into the night into the
darkness of her loss into the
darkness of what is ahead
with only a spark of light inside
at some time at some place
in a town somewhere
a bus station a mother takes
her children off a bus
walks with her children
to an address that says asylum

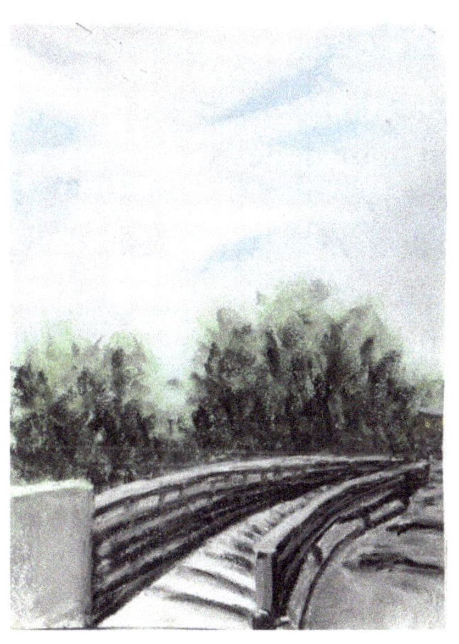

somewhere in her world of possibility
she has an address written in hope
an address for asylum
near the bus station somewhere an official office
with a flag of stripes and stars
she opens the door the threshold of a better life
for her and her children

she is questioned she speaks through an interpreter
she does not understand the questions
her children holding on to her
she is told that they need to be
taken care of will be taken care of
no one to trust no one's eyes meeting hers
her children are taken to another place
she is taken to a holding place
not knowing what has happened
or what will be?

the authorities act with out emotion
acting on orders from above
just another asylum seeker trying to bring
her children across the border
defending their actions with decrees from higher ups
forgetting their childhood their mothers their fathers
defending their callousness with a job to be done
forgetting the opportunities they were given
defending their salaries the pensions that they have
forgetting their rooms their schools their teams
defending their earned positions of authority
forgetting the source of their connections
to the common striving of everyone every family
        mothers and daughters
        sons and fathers

circumstantial authoritarians in uniforms
defending the borders of their indifference
with the laws of abstraction and exclusion
justifying their unconscionable actions
ultimately forgetting who they are

within the greater family

within the core of their humanity

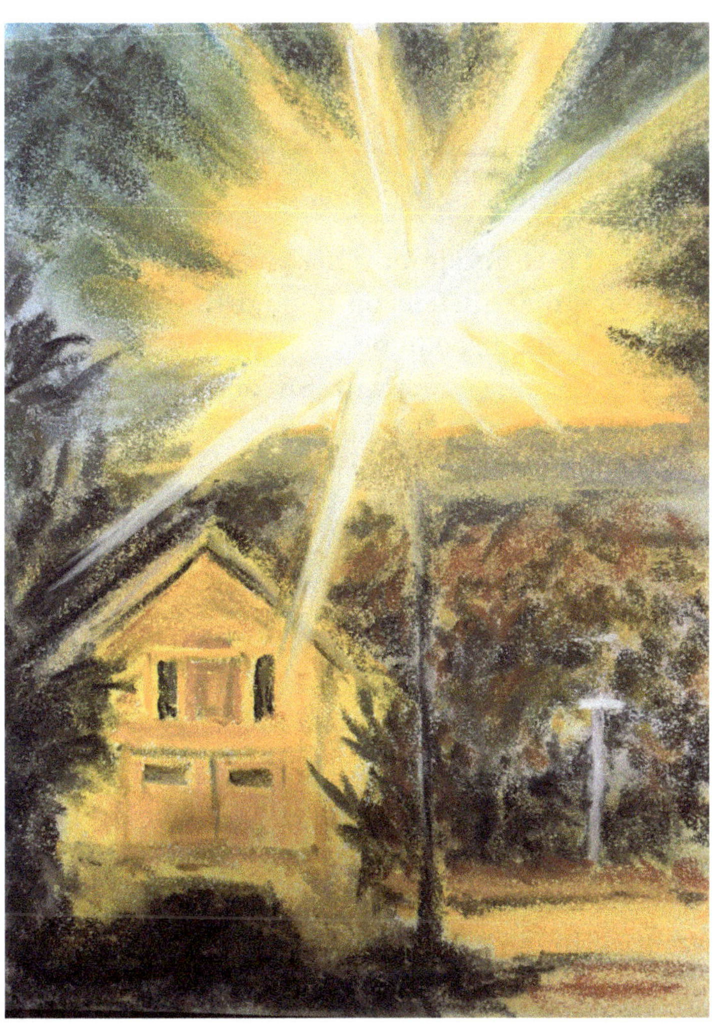

all the years
before us
all the years
that our mothers held us
all the years
that our fathers fought for us
that came before us
the ones so long gone long gone

let them go
if you can
let them go
into that cosmic memory
let them go
with a wind that invigorates the air
into a stream that glistens on it's swirling way
  to a world that used to be
a time that was once innocent inherent
  once wild once free

be the man
of the hour
be the woman

I think I know you
I think I know what you believe in
I think I know what you were born into
  where you came from
I think I know that your heart is wrapped up
  in the dying of a loved one
  wrapped in the anguish that aches
  and won't let go
I know that
I've been there

and sometimes the loss is overwhelming
the loss is too much
so hard to let go
I know that my dear friend
I know that

pray to your gods
pray to the heaven's that you believe in
   if you need to
pray until you realize the created gods
   of our history
once set the creative forces in motion

and here we are
the culmination of all the years

here we are
still coming forth

just don't forget
the seeds of the earth
the love that gave you birth don't forget
the pomegranates bursting with blood red tartness
allowing us to live in the springtimes to come
allowing the rain to purge and restore us
the stream to flow and alleviate our thirst
the corn to grow crunchy and sweet
the beans to fill the tortillas
sticking to our mouth
the aroma of sun ripened tomatoes
becoming the salsa our mothers made

don't forget my traveling companion
when we commune at the local cantina
the tequila is spirited
the limes are tart

the salt on the glass brings out
the sea and the air
    allowing the sky to open
    ideas to be grasped
    purposes to be illuminated
    manifestos to be written
    justice to be fought for
    in the minds and streets

don't forget those photo albums
of yesteryear
now we have 10,000 images in our hand
to see who we once were
only yesterday
to see who we have not become
and who we have become
and who we are
too soon past
too soon gone
too soon out of sight
no stopping this
wheel of time
no stopping the life
that is yours
and mine

still we are so near

so close to another day

so close to all the years

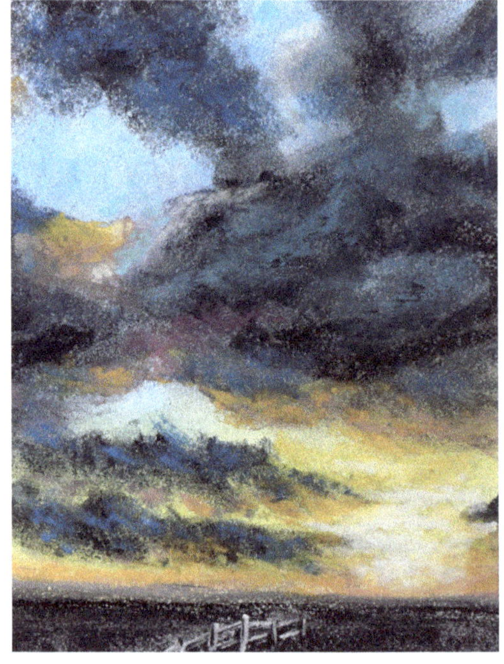

Paul Robeson
caught up in Hoover's paranoia
the commie hunt
passport taken
made a prisoner
in his own country
fighting for justice owed
he said let me sing
of the oppressed and segregated
and he sang to Canadians listening
words that crossed the border

Allen Ginsburg
when suburbs were breeding
and a cocktail
became home
a mind reeling
in a strange land
heard the midnight beats
he said let me speak
against conformity
and he sang of tigers burning bright
words that exposed borders

Joan Baez
singing in Club 47
folk stories
brought to life
eyes of laughter
voice of passion
on the cusp of concern
she said let me sing
for all that we need to change
and she sang to America
words that challenged borders

search for the voice that speaks for truth
search for the words that speak for all
let them sound with a deep conviction
to overcome our divisive walls

Paul Simon
in his poetry and music
heartfelt thoughts
manifesting
on Bleecker street
and the village green
in a dangling conversation
he said let me sing
of beauty and darkness
and he sang to those ready to question
the borders of our lives

Bucky Fuller
he almost drowned in despair
but found himself
in the secrets
of the universe
vowed to be a creator
for all humanity
he said let me sing
of nature's structures
and he sang 50 years into the future
ideas transcending borders

Bob Dylan
from the hard scrabble midwest
New York bound
he found Woody dying
in a fertile mist
ear to the ground
absorbed in sound
he said let me sing
of the times and the wind
and he sang to a new generation
words with no borders known

Leonard Cohen
immersed in the spoken word
Canadian born
culturally tuned
with a "golden voice"
filled his poetry
with music
he said let me sing
of love and freedom
and he sang to all the searching hearts
words overcoming borders

Martin Luther King
marching out of the shadows
Washington bound
felt the injustice
years of struggle
filled the oppressed
with hope
he said let me speak
of change through non violence
and he spoke to all of America's people
words to break the borders

search for the voice that
speaks for truth

search for the words that
speak for all

let them sound
with a deep conviction

to overcome our divisive
walls

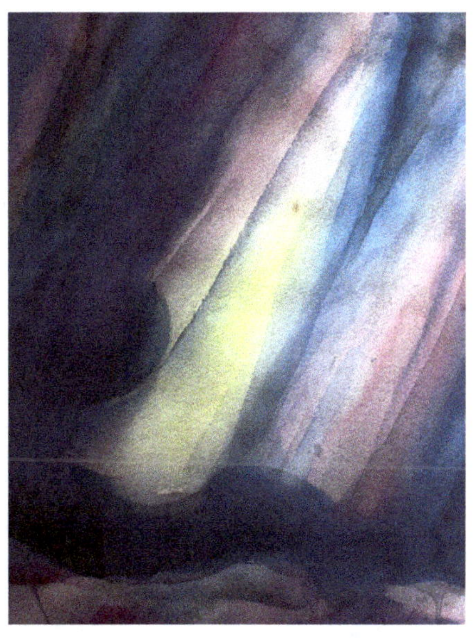

days of revolution
can be found in 1911
in the area of Schwabing
where artists found their place
Kandinsky came from Russia
    painting knights on horseback
    proclaiming the spiritual in art
Franz Marc was a local
    painting cows in primal blue
Schoenberg let the tones decide
    how  the octaves would divide
Klee played violin
    and drew the world in lines
he and Macke soaked in Tunisia
finding colors in the sun

days of revolution
can be found in devastation in the
    after math of the "great" war
    and the amputated sons
Grosz saw misery and horror
    and exposed the greed and
    futility of human errors
Gropius saw potential
in the crippled cultural rubble
   and the bauhaus was born
to begin again with radical intentions
to build the house and shelter
the structures of our public life
in refined material and design
for our modern times

days of revolution
in the heady days of Paris
seducing writers and artists
to dive into the milieu
Picasso painted Mademoiselles of Avignon
Hemingway wrote "a moveable feast"
Dali melted time and brought elephants to ride
Cocteau let loose "the blood of a poet"
and Gertrude brought them all together
there was a there there

days of revolution
Rudolf Steiner's vision of man and epochs
brought the esoteric into sculptural cement
the Goetheanum rose in Dornach
Faust found redemption
eurythmy found its movement
given life inside the hall
of planetary columns
surrounding all
who ventured into the
cosmic meaning
of humanity
streaming out of his
clairvoyant view
initiatives born
lectures given
verses written
for the seasons
and these
Michaelic times

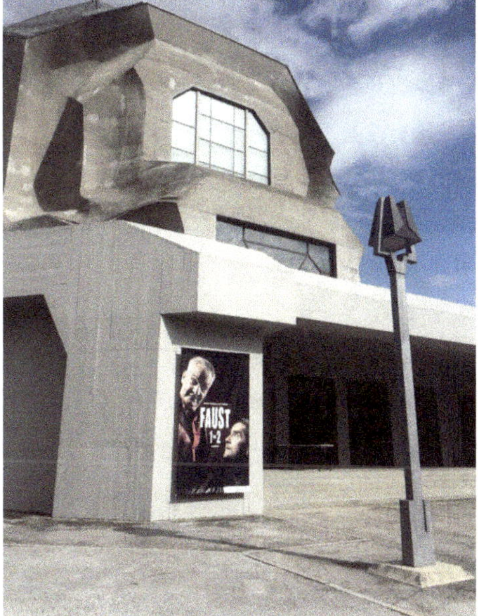

days of revolution
on an evening ride to Sausalito
stopping at a carriage house
to view the momentous news
the great undoing of the world's division
the Berlin wall was breached and coming down
the symbol of a nuclear standoff
missiles aimed and ready
now the incredible had happened
people rose up within authoritarian silence
and possible brutal response
they broke through the fences
climbed the barbed bricks of the wall
stood in exaltation on that painful history
stood and laughed and sang
silhouetted against the sky
stood and cried in the light of freedom
without a shot fired without a life lost that day
a miracle of the inevitable spirit of the many
and the wisdom of a few
who had the power at their command

days of revolution
the new age came on without knowing
after Satchmo had blown the trumpet
and take five had been taken
someone howled into the smoke
the ancient story tellers were
becoming new again were a-changing
the beats in the rhythms and the blues
were being amplified by the rocking bands
rocking far out sprung out playing into the night
until the sound spread across america
so many pied pipers and tambourines
hare Krishna hare hare

a new gen gen gen generation
questioning the worth of their comforts
  the reasons for their dying
  in some foreign jungle
black light posters paisley shirts
joints smoked acid taken patterns projected
  on walls and minds and dancers
street protests and borders questioned
  peace brother sister
in the hearts of many
once upon a timeless now

days of revolution
in the land of the brave and free
now so murky and divisive
from underground resentment
years of rage and hate
breaching the light of day
awakening the perplexed with sadness felt
and the internet of such potential
being questioned derided over by fake truth
  discourse shouted down stories mired in
  stereotypes and labels
who knows what this will come to mean
in the history of this america...
  as town criers of old are now connected
  and projected into cities farms towns suburbs
  proclaiming the warnings of conflicts and
  the silencing of voices

all in contrast to the millions of people in the
  world waking rising reaching grasping...
  so hungry for opportunity...

while lady liberty still stands and steps towards the future
with the arms and hands of generosity and inclusion
her spirit gracing the harbor of the eastern coast
and the golden gate of the west
and the vast expanse of the north
and the many dreams of the south

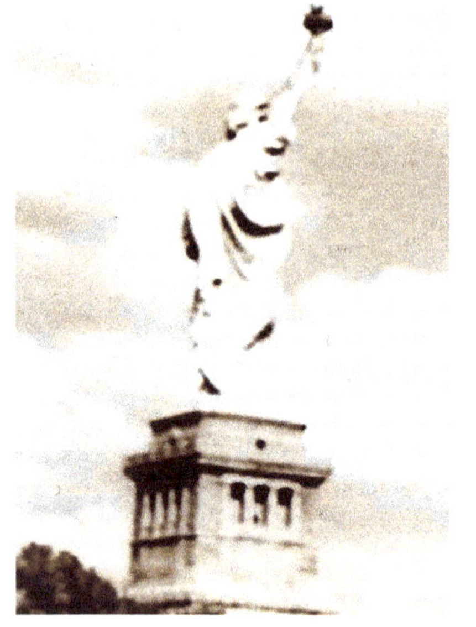

individual goodwill still
reaching out and on going
with compassion
acknowledgment
and justice
still being fought for
and lived for
within this human dialectic
within this historic time

this intersection of past
and future ages

converging in

becoming these

days of
revolution

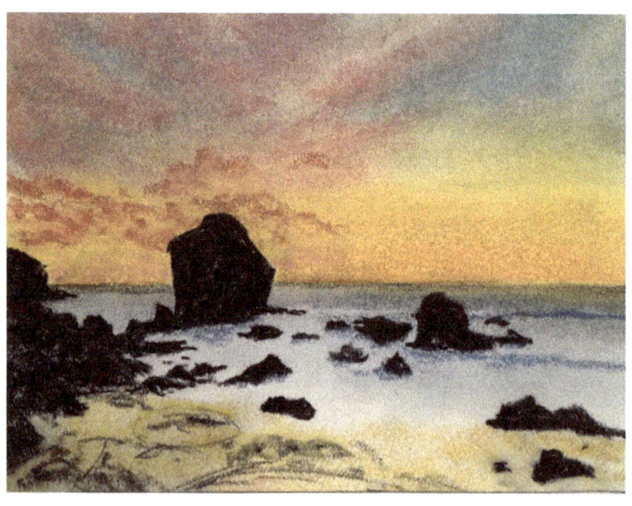

## *a new democracy*

*thoughts of freedom forming*

it's a new democracy
so new that you can't see
it's a love of freedom
that was many times fought over
and sometimes debated and so
 eloquently written up
it's a story of almost there you see
remember the seeds that were buried
 so long ago
those that sprouted in a fertile land
those that took hold in the ground
 red with blood
taken by force from the native people
in the midst of cruelty thousands died
without shame without a name
the bodies buried in a river of tears
sorrow living on and on

expand your vision
widen the circles of your home
the familiar that you were born into
and have known
widen and expand
make connections not seen before
felt before
one door at a time
one walkway to the gate
one fence to climb over
one wall that you can look over
one handshake of acknowledgement
when this pandemic is overcome
one communion with a neighbor
one man walking his dog in the morning
one hello one more to go

it's a new democracy
what was owned by the inherited elite
became a timely historical dialectic
that the world had waited for was ready for
the dreams of those who signed the declaration
the dreams of those who declared that
  "all men are created equal"
  is a story of almost there...
as destiny gripped the minds and the land
we remember the subjugation of Africans
taken from their homes their land their ancestors
being bought and sold without rights or recourse

until the country went into the abyss
breaking apart trembling shuddering
with the bloodied clash of bayonets
the bloody fields of wailing and dying
sorrow living on and on

expand your vision
enlarge the circle of your life
the familiar that you were born into
and have known
widen and expand
make connections not seen before felt before
one walk in a new neighborhood
one bench in a public park
one float in a parade
one festival of music and transformation
one organized march in sought after change
one gathering in nature's glory and wildness
one view over the border over the wall
one exploration of another life
one visa to go

it's a new democracy
so new that we can't see
there are still thoughts of freedom
once fought for died for and now being
trumped trampled and divided
individual rights and privacy churning in the
cauldron of extremes and economic disparities
and accumulated conveniences
remember the sacrifices of the last century
recognize the challenges of this one
the world wide web of our evolution
will affect all our children to come
incredible changes living on and on

expand your vision
enlarge the circle of your life
the familiar that you were born into
and have known
widen and expand
make connections not seen before felt before
one child in the shadows
one teacher to inspire and question
one hand reaching out to another
one act that overcomes despair and distrust
one sacrifice for our living systems
one attempt to solve our living needs
one search for the truth again
one smile to go

it's a new democracy
so new that we can try to imagine
it's a love of freedom
that rises out of who we are

**who we can still**
**remember to be...**

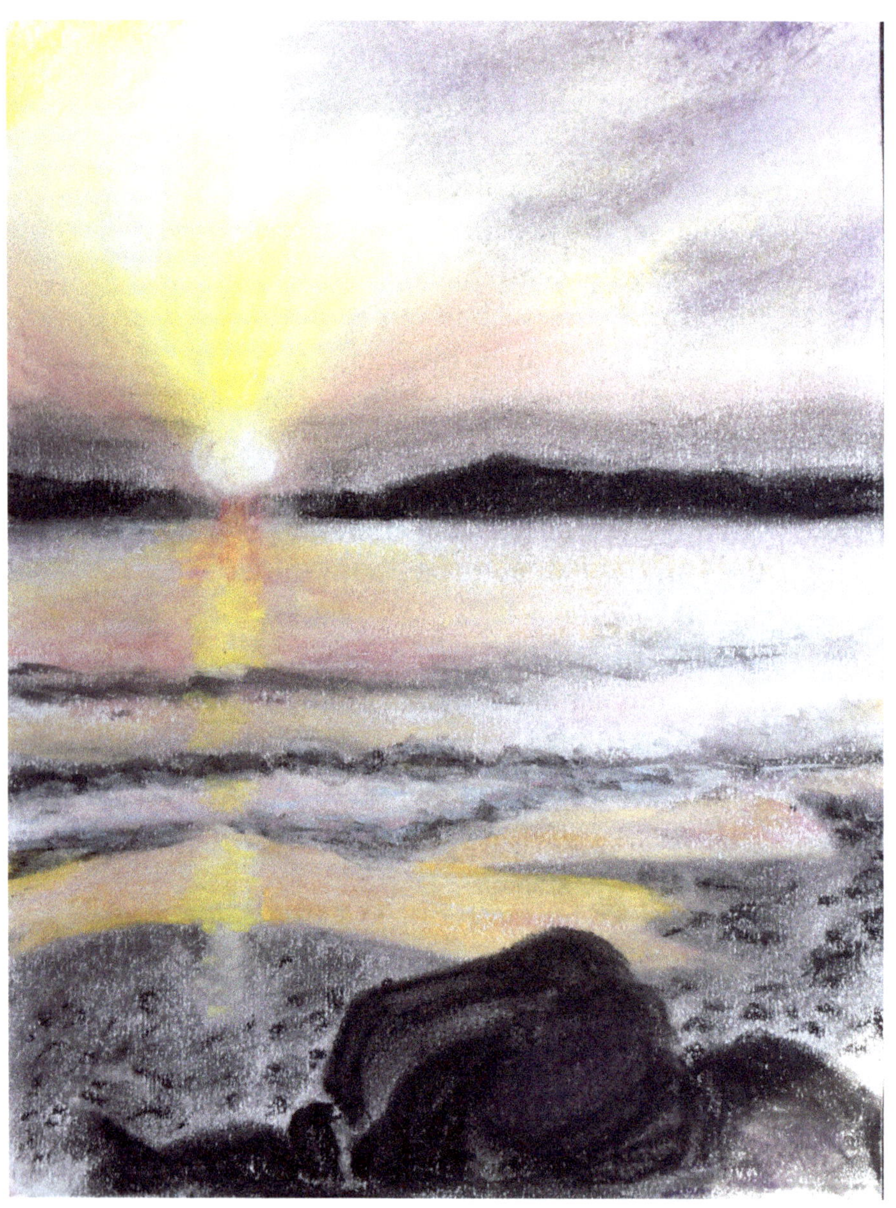

to write
to reap the words
so wrought in pain and desperation
so clothed in warmth and momentary comfort
cursing breath and blood
yet tendered in care and love
cherished in thoughts and deeds
cultivated and coaxed out of the
    seeds of knowledge
so raised in a child's realm of touch
so flowing in our atmosphere of being
so blooming in our glory

to write
to grasp the words
emerging out of late night wanderings
and down solitary paths as we
once flagellated our sinewy sensuous backs
with cuts and blows from hand made whips
to cast out our proverbial sins
until our souls were raw and bleeding
to overcome the wrath of our deeply held
troubling traditions and mythologies

to write
to continue the words
so inflamed with fear and reaction
the brutality of the righteous
the narrow mind of the self righteous
the words mouthed in hate
that drive some to random cruelty
that drive some to separate and exclude
to render abstract to number another human being
that allows horrors to happen

to write
and now to castigate
on so called social media
without consequence or responsibility
without seeing the face of another
seeing their eyes
hearing their sometimes desperate cries

to write
to remember
and to elevate the language
of our history
with the earliest reminders of love for someone
for friends for our families our offspring

to write
to steep in
the aromas of spring time
the cutting of grass
and the reaping of wheat
for the awesome movement of the stars
the awakening of the dawn of a day
our breath in the midst of a forest
water in the depths of a desert
the glory of our structures
reaching into the heavens of our abilities
our learned and practiced skills
creating a spoon or drawing in a sacred cave

to write
and bring the words to a child
infusing an abstract layer of understanding
into every birth and generation
the beginning of our earthly intelligence
    out of the realm of the senses

we gave the world a name
we give it numbers
now is the time of our transformation
the colliding of our cultures
the time of our fears and
our exhilarations

to write
to speak
to live our words
to become who we are
to become what we can be

and still remember
the stories written down
so long ago
still in our gut and our thoughts
still inspiring
so long ago

still transforming

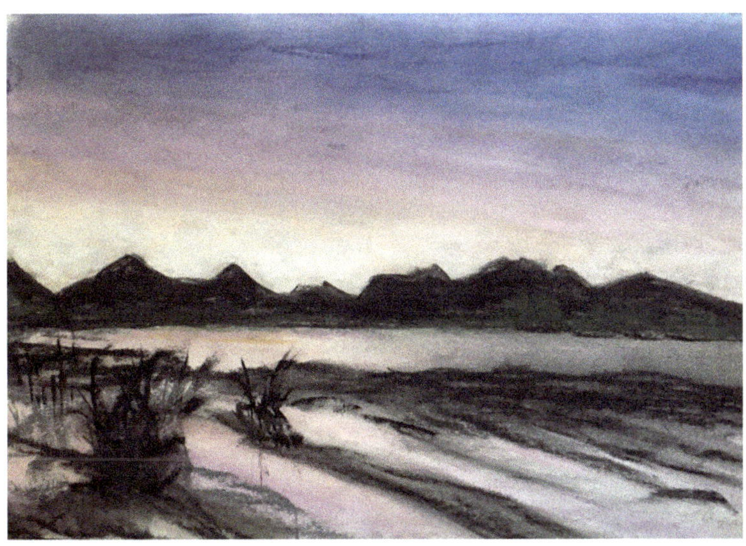

through words written I was transformed
realizations born a path forward
emerging from the storm

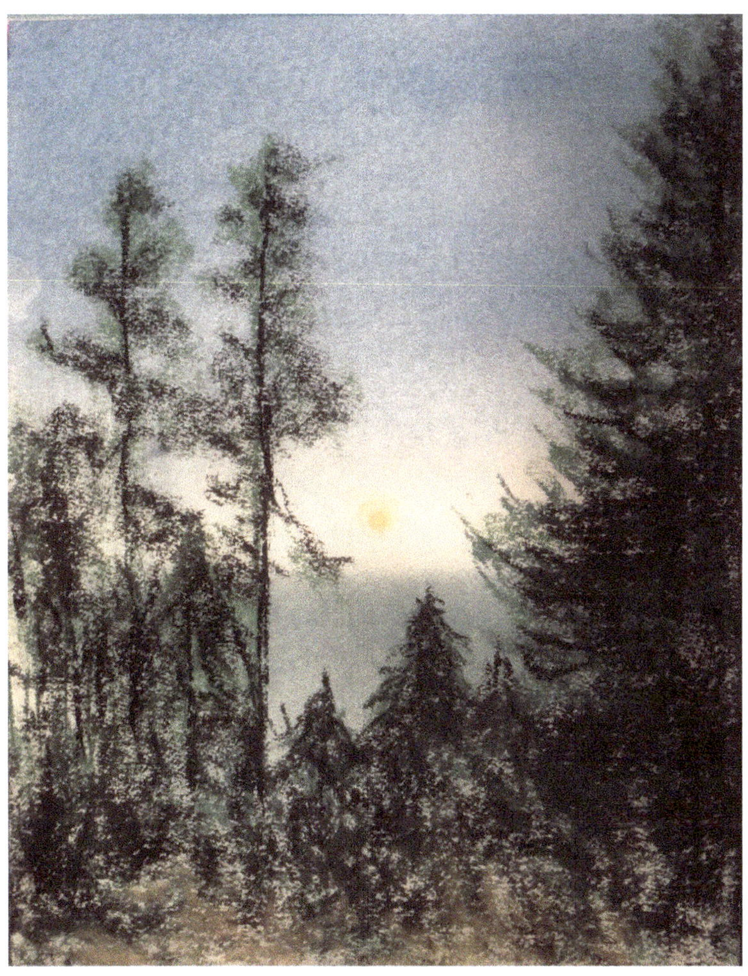

# in the midst

I draw with chalk
with colored strokes and dabs and smudges
feel the images in their expression and possibility
their glory their subtlety
their chiaroscuro of contrasts their depths
let their particular emergence arise
out of our perceived world…

I draw with chalk
and smudge the colors
draw the lines
form the shadows
and values
try to keep the light
the amazing transience
of the light
a reminder that beauty may
just be beauty
because of those fleeting
moments in our lives
impossible to hold onto
yet captured on a wall
a canvas a pattern of pixels
a page of a pastel pad

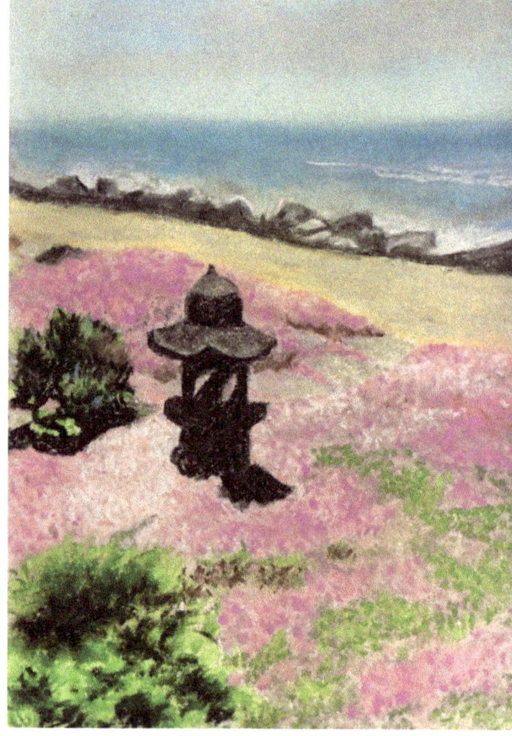

somehow somewhere
in an intersection of
occurrences a future showing is prepared
being matted and framed and saved on a screen
for the world's eyes to take in to grasp to feel
in whatever way the images may penetrate
and unite and combine and
fill our existence…

## *the tide*

the tide has washed away
our proverbial castles on the beach
that took us so long to build
they've all washed away
  the parapets the towers the seaweed garden
  the eighth wonder of Half Moon Bay
they've all sunk out of reach
  the drift wood lintels the sea green glass
they've all scattered in the sun
  even the deep dug moat has been overcome
we have our hands
yet hesitancy comes on
holding us in place
the waves are relentless
riptides wait in the depths
our legs stand sink
while the moon seduces the vast ocean
into rising slowly to inundate and
erase our remaining foot prints
our minds imagine want desire
to reach downward to build a more solid foundation

to walk to feel the sand between our toes
to wonder what will stay and what will be washed away
  see the scattered driftwood
smoothed by the grinding grains and the salty sea
stacked by the hands of some youthful dreamer
become a sanctuary in the afternoon sunlight
streaming through the openings
streaming into a hallowed space
of seasoned and embracing wood
become nature's transient transformation
as we sit and take our turn and
listen to the incessant surf coming ever closer

how our minds have devised systems
of defense a moat a wall a thousand miles long
weapons of defense and ironic destruction
to realize the shelters we've made
with all their structural integrity
and all their encompassing beauty
their crafts and arts displayed
transcendent in the spaces made

do we have the will
to stack the stones the bricks
to raise the beams and glass
to build the houses domes and towers
do we have the hunger and desire to build
with our living systems in mind
   the sand is here the driftwood awaits
   the seaweed is left behind
   see the sparkle of smoothed sea green glass

we are born into this earthly state
into the pulsing of our heart
moments of our fleeting joy
bring meaning to our existence
even as we cry out for life
when brutal acts erupt and try to eradicate
every remnant of love connecting us
leaving nothing but madness and pain

how do we ignite the flame
inside our heart our brain
rekindle the will to start again
when all the gods have looked away
and the scriptures still preach sacrifice
and the myths still narrate the meaning of life
with our hopes still tossed on the funeral pyre
   of deadly conflagrations and

so many still hang onto born beliefs
after the centuries of observation between
heretical burning and the physical understanding
of our earthly and cosmic connections
what can we still believe in
what can we still work for
how can we find some future in all of this
when mortal man and woman
    scream into the night
when visceral reactions erupt in blind fury
    turn brutal and indifferent
where do we go when this small planet
this dot in our galaxy with its own orbiting moon
and its life giving star falls apart breaks down becomes
unrecognizable unbearable inhospitable
is washed away lost in the great ocean of our nightmares

will a child still have time to play
    on this breaking upending changing beach
will their life filled bodies still rush in run back out
    with the movement of the waves
not realizing the over riding lunar force
that has influenced and changed the edges
    of our lands and seas over millennia of time
a cosmic gravity that does not depend on earthly love
or the beauty of earthly arts
or desperation or despair
or desperate belief

will there still be a place
for play and reaching out and digging deep
and running in and out of the past and future
    when all innocence is gone
    when all endeavors have washed away
will the hands of some youthful dreamer
still build a sanctuary in the afternoon sunlight?

yesterday

the knight of mirrors
came calling again

just when I thought I had left him
on some battle ground diminished in power
strewn around

just when I thought I had shattered
that reflection into broken pieces
no description

just when I thought I had taken on the
gauntlet of a cause it snapped in two
action on pause

just when I thought I had pulled out
the sword of the will handle broken
my force stilled

just when I thought I was working
on ideals and beauty the ground gave way
a muddy sea

yesterday

the knight of mirrors
came calling again

just when I thought I had shored up
the precarious rock the sand bar changed
land was dark

just when I thought I was engaged
in future works no inner resolve
kept me on track

just when I thought I had escaped
the maw of the void the suction
too strong to avoid

just when I thought I had grasped
a grand notion I tasted the cup
a dark potion

yesterday

the knight of mirrors
came calling again

just when I thought I was overcome
by dark reflections and shards of shame
redemption came

through words written I was transformed
realizations born a path forward
emerging from the storm

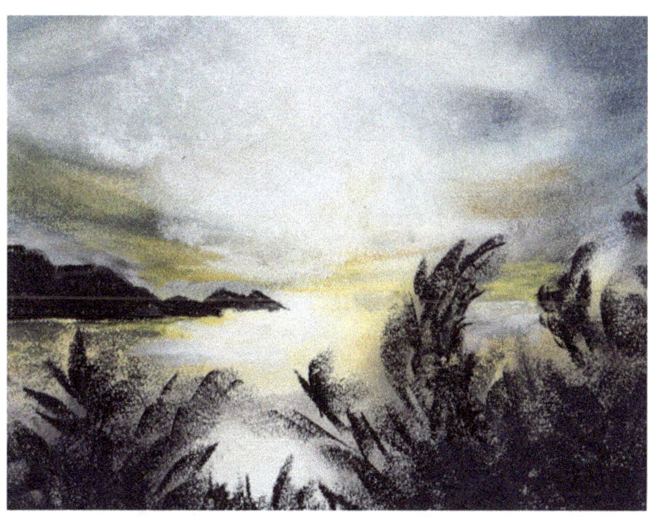

we are so small against
the stars
and yet so large in our
imagination

we have created the abstract relationships
of constellations and mined our DNA
generated binary numbering and formative formulas
realized the positions of our time and space
our cosmic place
recognized the vastness of our past
our awareness of the future
yes this is who we are

we are so small against
the stars
and yet so conscious
of our overcoming

we have succumbed to the worst
in ourselves
brought about
inconceivable cruelty
and suffering
and yet we have risen from
the horrors and the ashes
we have healed the wounded
and buried the dead
we have piled up the bricks
and swept the streets
once oozing in red
yes this is who we are

we have lived with despair
through our losses and our sadness
and our existential madness
only to be replaced with
the sound of a new born child
crying for life a mother's pain now
felt in the joy of creation
    yes this is who we are

we are filled with the sound
of voices singing out of desperation
born in struggle calling out
with soulful response and ancient wailing
a gospel choir stirring provoking
singing the heartfelt hallelujah
    yes this is who we are

        we are so small against
        the stars
        and yet so large in our
        dreams and desires

the will to continue
within every hard fall every loss
within every compulsion to stand up to rebuild
within every why of cancerous growth
within the cupped hands holding the seedlings
for the next generation
    yes this is who we are

        we are so small against
        the stars
        and yet so large
        in our history

in our stories transcribed
in the myths that we remember
the heroes of their time
carved in marble and on painted frescoes
the mothers of creation
bringing life onto the earth
the artists of all our ages
bringing beauty into ourselves
and into the world
    yes this is who we are

        we are so small against
        the stars
        and yet so large
        in our defiance

in our determination to survive
within the coursing of our blood
to the extensions of our minds
formulating our existence
with our hands
    crafting the logic board and
    manipulating the genetic record
    splitting the atoms of formation
    yes this is who we are

        we are so small against
        the stars
        and yet so vulnerable
        in our time

in the futures we've imagined
in the apocalyptic warnings
the gathered data of our earthly systems
extrapolated from observations

dire consequences virtually expressed
and horrendously experienced
living with our accumulated decisions
living with our accumulated disasters
the inferno in Paradise
the annihilation of Hiroshima
    yes this is who are

        we are so small against
        the stars
        and so miraculous
        in our existence

waking up again
to the streaming of the light
celebrating the turning of the earth
out of the relenting darkness
celebrating the solstice day
the moment of our cosmic changing
the transforming of our human existence
    love found in a child's laughter
    love found in the awakening of youth
    love found in our devotion and commitment
    in the living of our lives

yes this is who we are

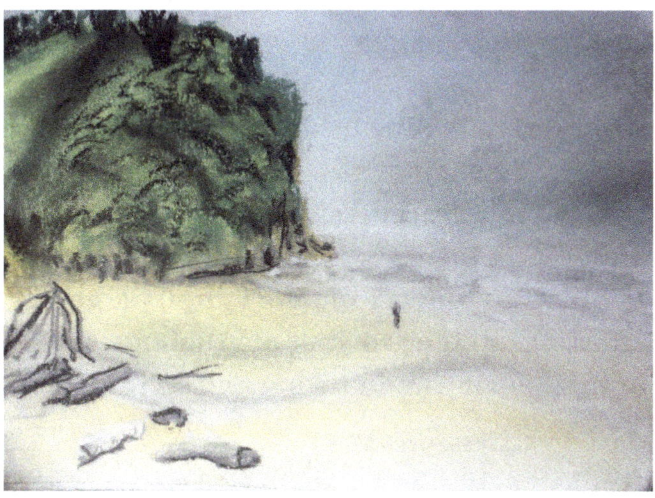

## *ode to mountain joy*

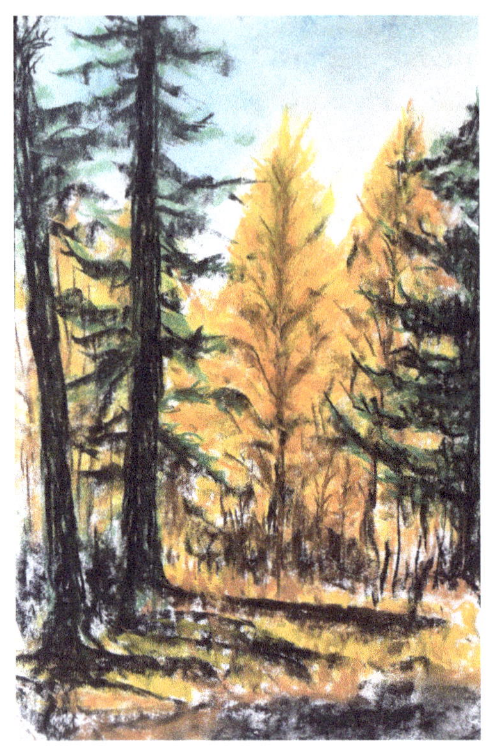

now
sitting here in made up
comfort perched upon the
wooded hillside
watching and listening
I have become part of a
consecrated mountain
symphony
resting and rushing
through its movements
on the edge of a designated
wilderness and the
hum of traffic on highway 89
curving around Lake Tahoe

witness to nearby Emerald Bay and the Vikingsholm
all under this blue dome of a cloudless sky

a flittering of light and shade opens the
first movement
the aspen leaves begin their quick staccato
shaking and quaking

while a stately pine in shadowed repose waits
for its moment
to bring in a graceful slow swaying
underlying theme
as the wind blows from the mountain height
affecting all the growing instruments
in their flexing and bowing and solidity

the manzanitas slightly tremble
a buzzing fly flits in and out
a high treble tweet a blue jay's squawk
while the out crops of granite move very slowly
in the eons of time

now
and then silence enters and a great stillness is felt
and again a great shifting and
blowing of the wind returns
like Beethoven's never ending endings
until we are filled and spent and ready
to contribute some of our own movements
some of our own staggering ideas and
grand notions
to this mountain setting
something we deeply feel
something needing to be done
someone wanting to be loved
some unchangeable tragic experience
a reality to be carried and worn as only we can
as only we are capable of bearing
in our acceptance
in our overcoming
in our chorus of never endings
in the unfolding
of our
lives

## *something still burns*

*prelude*

*a Maasai village with young men in red plaid blankets hover over the hands of one twirling a stick into a cedar board turning one way then the other twirling into that board until a wisp of smoke emerges, dried curled leaves are then gently added as the breath of life is finely blown into this mixture evoking prometheus until finally magically a flame appears…*

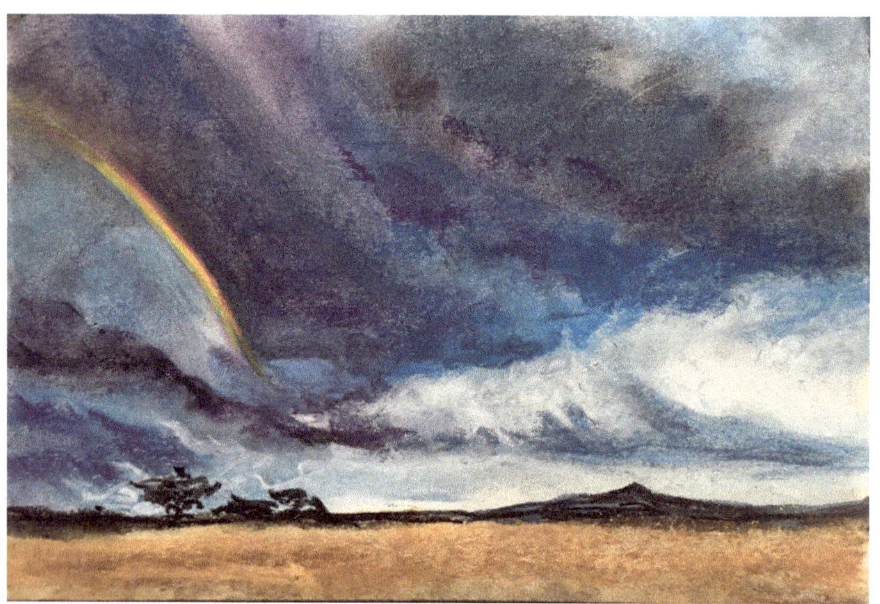

**something still burns in the fire of my heart**
**no matter how rough the night**
**or how unsettled**
**my sleep**

they twirl a stick
until a wisp of smoke comes out of the heat
add some dried dung or grass from the field
they blow on the embers
they share with their neighbors

I twirl a stick into the recesses
of my brain
twirl away twirl again
until a wisp of a moment
begins to emerge
small treasures of long ago thoughts and
momentary awareness begin to take shape
in such a swirling transcendent way

the *"Moonlight Sonata"* in a late evening bar
a walk on the strand in the twilight of the day
a historic work of reflection in *"Les Demoiselles*
*d'Avignon"*
a video of *"help me make it through the night"*
an anthem of *"birds singing at the break of day,*
*start again, I heard them say"*

don't let the world extinguish your flame
by the many who project their limited views
who get caught up in dread
and fear and hate and bigotry
they can shout it
they can claim that its theirs
they can lose themselves
they can feel secure
they may goose step to it
in one marching sound
they may foment their views
in ubiquitous constructs
while the paths to their source
take circuitous ways

don't let the world extinguish your flame
by the few who abuse and wield power
  threaten your inspired life
  with a knock on a midnight door
  with a fist or a gun

choose your path well
choose friends who inspire
and fill you with confidence
  when you're house is in flames
  when reason is lost
when despair meets you in a dark alley
  or the grim reaper meets you on a beach
or you're at an intersection of mirrors
  wondering who you've become
or which way to go
when the night closes in

don't let the world extinguish your flame
no matter where you end up
or how heavy the load
on your back or your mind
or your tomorrow

choose your love well
if you have a choice
because love and desire
can burn bright for a while
can light up your being
can bring on a morning
of dreams and beginnings
that you won't be able
to let go or go by

don't let the world extinguish your flame
it just takes a small group of group think
to obliterate your truth
    ignore the venal voice
    overcome the saber tongue

come out
twirl away twirl again
dancing singing with the sound unfurling
moving wondering imagining the world
until small treasures of long ago thoughts
begin to ignite begin to emerge
in such a swirling transcendent way

a walk around the Parthenon in sunlit glory
the momentous power of Yosemite Falls
    in the springtime
the candlelight voices in Grace Cathedral
the vast life of the wild in the Maasai Mara
an anthem for the new generations to come

*"an age of change is now upon us*
*a fight for justice is before us*
*the search for truth will now restore us*
*our time has just begun..."*

something still burns in the fire of my heart
no matter how low the flames go
how vague and dim the light

something still burns in the fire of my heart...

# Postlude

*the word becoming*

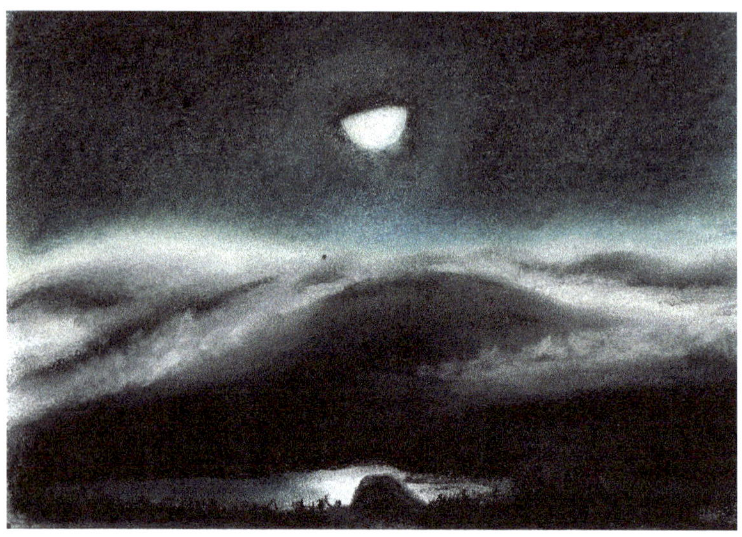

the word on a sign a symbol a page
the word spoken now written
the word of the heavens
formed on the earth
the creation begun
within the evolution of the cosmos
the turning of time and energy amassed and giving birth
all human history changed when
the words were carved and stamped
and drawn on walls and scrolls
words to read back and repeat
    after stories were forgotten
    after fireside stories were left behind
new generations carried their stories and
    history with them
        the arks of belief
        the lore and wisdom
        becoming the arcs of history

written words became sacred
sometimes many times unyielding
sometimes to name the unseen
sometimes a reminder on steles and arches
of grand deeds conquering exploits brutal acts

somewhere words became songs
sung over the rhythms of rattles and drums
sung and sounded in full moon night
in a fireside gathering
in a sunrise awakening
in a harvest's reaping
carried within a painted wagon rolling
into another village another valley
into the courts of circumstantial kings
words became the language
of poets bards minstrels
some lost over time
some written down over time
the words of cultural unfolding
ballads and stories becoming
the thoughts the ideas the expressions
of evolving communities
and the love songs of intimate heart felt feelings
take just one song
made up of the word and words
so apprehensively chosen
so sought after and mined
carefully selected
finally laid bare
a revelation of words spewing forth
a Dionysian birth again and again
out of pain and dance becoming myth
out of need out of will out of desire
the placement of the words becoming

their context construed
spoken at gatherings and
illuminated in manuscripts
written and printed in books
of great import
and dime store novellas
written with voices in mind
words to be sung with stories to behold
when childhood begins and
adolescence soaks up every breath and sound
infused in emotion and felt
deep in the gut in the groin
in the heart of first love
and in the first heart rending loss
until a song of exhilaration surfaces again
until a world of wrong so obvious
breaks into an innocent view
injustice unexplained
until a word a song a voice comes out
that seems so necessary so right
the first awareness of youth
so written spoken sung in an ever vigilant fight

to write one word one poem one song
that enlightens the mind
that can brighten the night
and soothe the heart
that someone in what ever time of life
can return to and go back to again
can reach for in that moment of pain
and touch the well spring the source again
transcending desperation
          bringing exaltation and wonder
          through the touchstone of the word
              so long ago created

a poem a song an inspiration
a balm for the inner being
and the outer life
being lived
the word on a sign a symbol a page
a poem a book the word spoken
and sung
the word
becoming

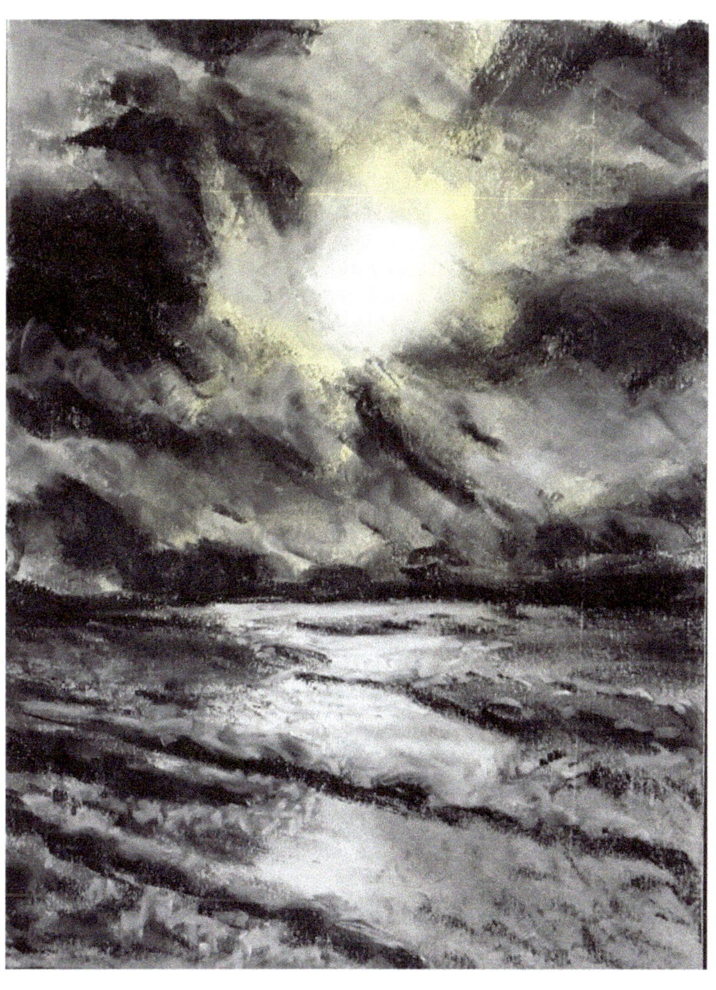

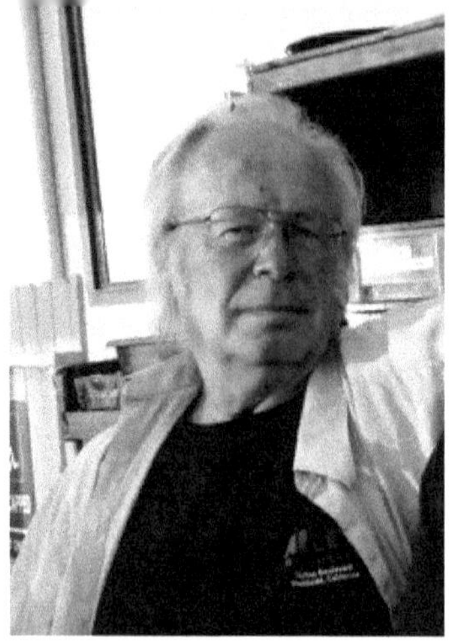

## hopes and dreams

to create
through the extensions of
our lives and arts

to imagine
out of our living circumstances
what is possible

to fulfill our capacities
as human beings
from compassion to action

to comprehend
the natural world we have inherited
and the universe we are a part of

to embrace
the ultimate aspects
of our humanity

to resonate
on the vibrational levels
of all existence

to continue
coming closer to the above

Rainer Neumann
02/02/2020

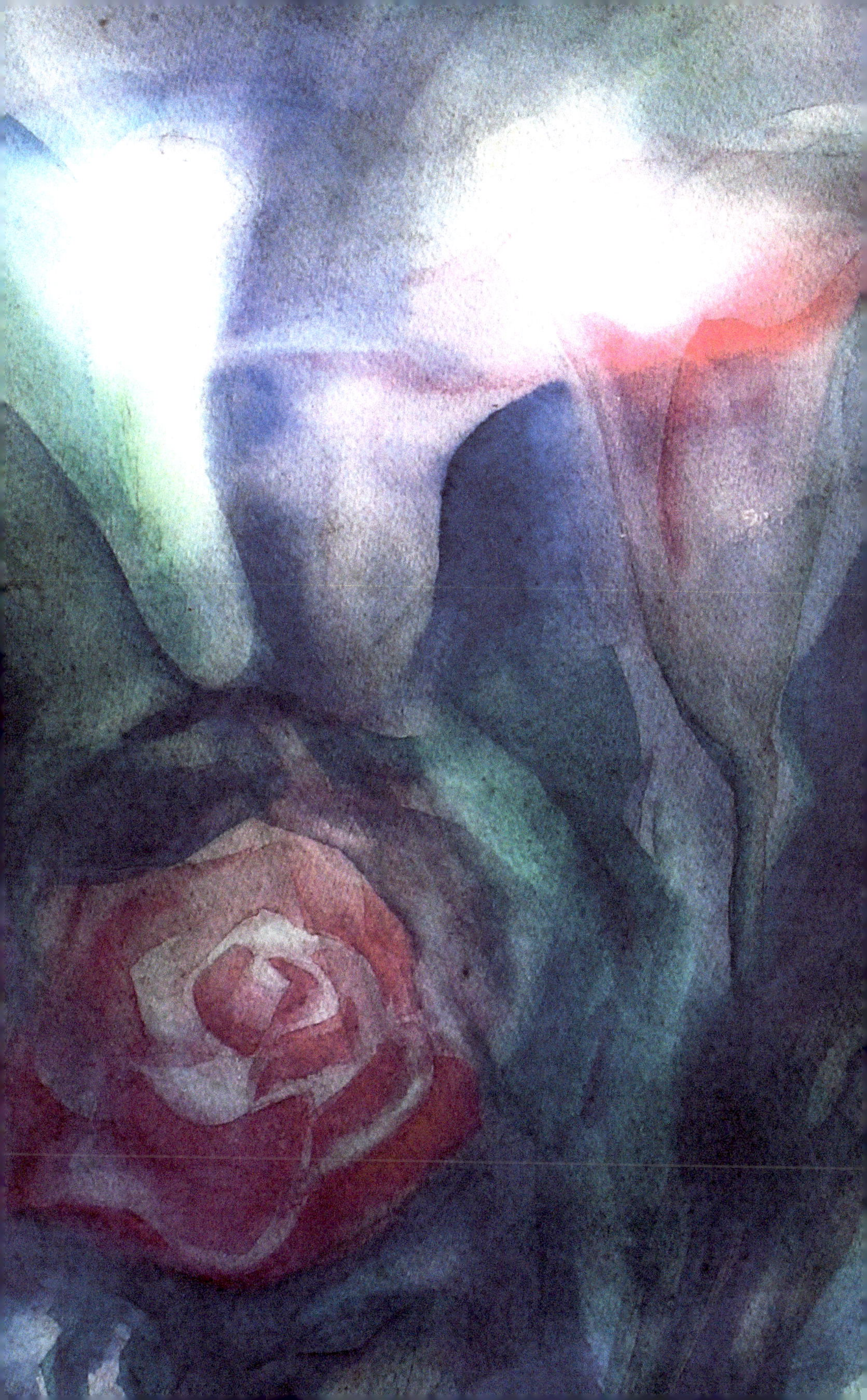

Exhibit Books

***from Pigeon Point to Point Reyes***

*pastel drawings and haikus*

***Homeland Serenity***

*pastel images and haikus from Half Moon Bay*

Books

***Our time has just Begun - a book of lyrics***

***Friday Night Jazzz***

***Masama***

***Labyrinth a mythic journey***

***Goodbye Bolinas we'll see you again***

***On the Wings of a Swan***

***Path and Goal***

*poetry by Alfred Neumann*

***I am always with you***

*a journal by Marianne Neumann*

both books translated by the author

Available through:

**lulu.com/spotlight/rneumann**

For further inquiries email:

**onhighwayone@gmail.com**

or see:

**landseandsky.com**

www.ingramcontent.com/pod-product-compliance
Lightning Source LLC
LaVergne TN
LVHW050538100826
845148LV00002B/597

* 9 7 8 0 5 7 8 7 2 8 9 8 8 *